Child Abuse
and Stress Disorders

Psychological Disorders

Psychological Disorders

Child Abuse and Stress Disorders

M. Foster Olive, Ph.D.

Consulting Editor
Christine Collins, Ph.D.
Research Assistant
Professor of Psychology
Vanderbilt University

Foreword by
Pat Levitt, Ph.D.
Vanderbilt Kennedy
Center for Research
on Human Development

CHELSEA HOUSE
PUBLISHERS
An imprint of Infobase Publishing

Child Abuse and Stress Disorders

Chelsea House
An imprint of Infobase Publishing
132 West 31st Street
New York NY 10001

Library of Congress Cataloging-in-Publication Data
Olive, M. Foster.
  Child abuse and stress disorders / M. Foster Olive ; foreword by Pat Levitt.
     p. cm. — (Psychological disorders)
  Includes bibliographical references and index.
  ISBN 0-7910-9006-X (hardcover)
  1. Stress in children. 2. Stress (Physiology) 3. Stress (Psychology) I. Title.
II. Series.
  RJ507.S77.O45 2007
  155.4'18—dc22   2006024071

Chelsea House books are available at special discounts when purchased in bulk quantities for businesses, associations, institutions, or sales promotions. Please call our Special Sales Department in New York at (212) 967-8800 or (800) 322-8755.

You can find Chelsea House on the World Wide Web at http://www.chelseahouse.com

Text and cover design by Keith Trego

Printed in the United States of America

Bang EJB 10 9 8 7 6 5 4 3 2 1

This book is printed on acid-free paper.

Table of Contents

Foreword

Pat Levitt, Ph.D.
Vanderbilt Kennedy
Center for Research
on Human Development

Think of the most complicated aspect of our universe, and then multiply that by infinity! Even the most enthusiastic of mathematicians and physicists acknowledge that the brain is by far the most challenging entity to understand. By design, the human brain is made up of billions of cells called neurons, which use chemical neurotransmitters to communicate with each other through connections called synapses. Each brain cell has about 2,000 synapses. Connections between neurons are not formed in a random fashion, but rather, are organized into a type of architecture that is far more complex than any of today's supercomputers. And, not only is the brain's connective architecture more complex than any computer, its connections are capable of *changing* to improve the way a circuit functions. For example, the way we learn new information involves changes in circuits that actually improve performance. Yet some change can also result in a disruption of connections, like changes that occur in disorders such as drug addiction, depression, schizophrenia, and epilepsy, or even changes that can increase a person's risk of suicide.

Genes and the environment are powerful forces in building the brain during development and ensuring normal brain functioning, but they can also be the root causes of psychological and neurological disorders when things go awry. The way in which brain architecture is built before birth and in childhood will determine how well the brain functions when we are adults, and even how susceptible we are to such diseases as depression, anxiety, or attention disorders, which can severely disturb brain function. In a sense, then, understanding how the brain is built can lead us to a clearer picture of the ways in which our brain works, how we can improve its functioning, and what we can do to repair it when diseases strike.

Brain architecture reflects the highly specialized jobs that are performed by human beings, such as seeing, hearing, feeling, smelling, and moving. Different brain areas are specialized to control specific functions. Each specialized area must communicate well with other areas for the brain to accomplish even more complex tasks, like controlling body physiology—our patterns of sleep, for example, or even our eating habits, both of which can become disrupted if brain development or function is disturbed in some way. The brain controls our feelings, fears, and emotions; our ability to learn and store new information; and how well we recall old information. The brain does all this, and more, by building, during development, the circuits that control these functions, much like a hard-wired computer. Even small abnormalities that occur during early brain development through gene mutations, viral infection, or fetal exposure to alcohol can increase the risk of developing a wide range of psychological disorders later in life.

Those who study the relationship between brain architecture and function, and the diseases that affect this bond, are neuroscientists. Those who study and treat the disorders that are caused by changes in brain architecture and chemistry are psychiatrists and psychologists. Over the last 50 years, we have learned quite a lot about how brain architecture and chemistry work and how genetics contribute to brain structure and function. Genes are very important in controlling the initial phases of building the brain. In fact, almost every gene in the human genome is needed to build the brain. This process of brain development actually starts prior to birth, with almost all the neurons we will ever have in our brain produced by mid-gestation. The assembly of the architecture, in the form of intricate circuits, begins by this time, and by birth, we have the basic organization laid out. But the work is not yet complete, because billions of connections form over a remarkably long period of time, extending through puberty. The brain of a child is being built and modified on a daily basis, even during sleep.

While there are thousands of chemical building blocks, such as proteins, lipids, and carbohydrates, that are used, much like bricks and mortar, to put the architecture together, the highly detailed connectivity that emerges during child-hood depends greatly upon experiences and our environ-ment. In building a house, we use specific blueprints to assemble the basic structures, like a foundation, walls, floors, and ceilings. The brain is assembled similarly. Plumbing and electricity, like the basic circuitry of the brain, are put in place early in the building process. But for all of this early work, there is another very important phase of development, which is termed experience-dependent development. During the first three years of life, our brains actually form far more con-nections than we will ever need, almost 40% more! Why would this occur? Well, in fact, the early circuits form in this way so that we can use experience to mold our brain archi-tecture to best suit the functions that we are likely to need for the rest of our lives.

Experience is not just important for the circuits that control our senses. A young child who experiences toxic stress, like phys-ical abuse, will have his or her brain architecture changed in regions that will result in poorer control of emotions and feel-ings as an adult. Experience is powerful. When we repeatedly practice on the piano or shoot a basketball hundreds of times daily, we are using experience to model our brain connections to function at their finest. Some will achieve better results than others, perhaps because the initial phases of circuit-building provided a better base, just like the architecture of houses may differ in terms of their functionality. We are working to understand the brain structure and function that result from the powerful combination of genes building the initial architecture and a child's experience adding the all-important detailed touches. We also know that, like an old home, the architecture can break down. The aging process can be particularly hard on the ability of brain circuits to function at their best because positive change comes less readily as we get older. Synapses may be lost and brain chemistry can change over time. The difficulties in understanding how architecture gets built are paralleled by the complexities of what happens to that architecture as we grow older. Dementia associated with brain deterioration as a complication of Alzheimer's disease, or memory loss associated with aging or alcoholism are active avenues of research in the neuroscience community.

There is truth, both for development and in aging, in the old adage "use it or lose it." Neuroscientists are pursuing the idea that brain architecture and chemistry can be modified well beyond childhood. If we understand the mechanisms that make it easy for a young, healthy brain to learn or repair itself following an accident, perhaps we can use those same tools to optimize the functioning of aging brains. We already know many ways in which we can improve the functioning of the aging or injured brain. For example, for an individual who has suffered a stroke that has caused structural damage to brain architecture, physical exercise can be quite powerful in helping to reorganize circuits so that they function better, even in an elderly individual. And you know that when you exercise and sleep regularly, you just feel better. Your brain chemistry and architecture are functioning at their best. Another example of ways we can improve nervous system function are the drugs that are used to treat mental illnesses. These drugs are designed to change brain chemistry so that the neurotransmitters used for communication between brain cells can function more normally. These same types of drugs, however, when taken in excess or abused, can actually damage brain chemistry and change brain architecture so that it functions more poorly.

As you read the series Psychological Disorders, the images of altered brain organization and chemistry will come to mind in thinking about complex diseases such as schizophrenia or drug addiction. There is nothing more fascinating and important to understand for the well-being of humans. But also keep in mind that as neuroscientists, we are on a mission to comprehend human nature, the way we perceive the world, how we recognize color, why we smile when thinking about the Thanksgiving turkey, the emotion of experiencing our first kiss, or how we can remember the winner of the 1953 World Series. If you are interested in people, and the world in which we live, you are a neuroscientist, too.

Pat Levitt, Ph.D.
Director, Vanderbilt Kennedy Center
for Research on Human Development
Vanderbilt University
Nashville, Tennessee

What Is Stress?

Jerry didn't like his social studies class or his teacher Mr. Springfield. He thought the subject was the most boring thing in the world, and Mr. Springfield was equally as boring. Jerry spent most of his time in class daydreaming about Amy, the attractive blonde who sat two seats in front of him. Jerry had been working up the nerve to ask Amy to the prom, but he usually found he didn't quite have the courage. He had finally decided he was going to take a chance and ask her right after class let out when Mr. Springfield sprang a pop quiz on the students. Jerry looked at the test blankly and didn't know a single answer. He knew he was going to fail, and became worried that Mr. Springfield would notify his parents of his failing grade, just like he had done last semester. At the end of the period, Jerry reluctantly turned in his exam, knowing he would get it back next week with a big red "F" written on it. To cheer himself up, Jerry approached Amy after class and, with a quiver in his voice, asked her to the prom. She said no. Disgusted by the double-whammy he had just received, Jerry cut the rest of his classes for the day. To get his aggressions out, he decided to turn up the car radio and go for a drive. When he got to his car, however, Jerry found that the window had been smashed and his stereo stolen. The outraged Jerry pounded the roof of his car with his fist.

People encounter things that cause them stress every day. Some—like stepping in chewing gum—are a nuisance, but are rather trivial in the grand scheme of things. Other events—like war, the September 11, 2001 terrorist attacks, the Asian tsunami of 2004, or Hurricane Katrina in 2005—are things that can change people for the rest of their lives. Whether big or small, stress is a part of life, and people vary widely in how they deal with it. Some people, for example, are bothered by slow traffic, whereas others see it as a convenient excuse to be late for something they didn't want to do in the first place.

DEFINITION OF STRESS

So what exactly is **stress**? Actually, there is no one definition. Most people think of stress as life's daily hassles and hardships, such as social, financial, family, and academic pressures. However, the word *stress* was originally used as an engineering term in the context of physical stress on materials, such as the force or pressure put on a building by very strong winds. In fact, the first definition of *stress* in *Webster's New World Dictionary* is "a strain or straining force, as in the force exerted upon a body that tends to strain or deform its shape." In the early 1900s, physiologist Dr. Walter Cannon first applied the word *stress* to the human body, and described it in terms of biological pressures on the body, such as being exposed to extreme heat or cold, pain, discomfort, lack of oxygen, or low blood sugar. Cannon also noted that stress could be emotional in nature, and he urged doctors to pay attention to all possible disturbances of a patient's body, including emotional stress, that might lead to illnesses.

Today, most definitions of stress refer to the hardships or afflictions that affect people, whether in daily life or in times of famine, poverty, war, or natural disaster. In fact, the *Oxford English Dictionary* notes that the word *stress* is a shortened form

Figure 1.1 Heavy traffic or rude drivers are a common source of stress, which can sometimes build up into road rage. © *Anthony Redpath/CORBIS*

of the word *distress*. Things that cause us stress are often referred to as **stressors**. Most mental health professionals use the term *stress* to describe events that are stressful, but more importantly, to refer to the way those events make us feel. In other words, stress is a normal part of how people cope with the demands (whether physical or psychological) that are placed on them.

THE BIOLOGY OF THE STRESS RESPONSE

Although it is most often thought of as psychological in nature, stress produces very distinct and reliable physiological changes in the body. The majority of these physiological changes involve increased activity of certain divisions of the nervous system, and the production and secretion of hormones such as cortisol and adrenaline.

Cortisol

Whether the source of stress is emotional or physical in nature, the human body (and that of other mammals as well) has well-programmed, strategic biological mechanisms for responding to and coping with stress (Figure 1.2). When the brain receives information that it perceives as stressful, it causes a substance called **corticotrophin-releasing hormone** (CRH; also called corticotrophin-releasing factor, or CRF) to be released into the **pituitary gland**, which is located at the base of the brain. When cells in the pituitary gland are stimulated by CRH, they, in turn, release **adrenocorticotropin releasing hormone** (ACTH) into the bloodstream. This occurs within a minute or so of the stressful event. ACTH travels in the blood to the adrenal glands, which are located directly above the kidneys. There it stimulates the production and release of the stress hormone **cortisol** into the bloodstream. This occurs about five minutes after the stressor is noted.

Once cortisol, which is chemically classified as a **steroid**, is released into the bloodstream, it causes various physiological changes to help us adapt to stress. First, cortisol can increase the activity of the **immune system**, improving the body's ability to fight off any infections or intrusions by viruses or bacteria. Although this is useful in the short term, long-term stress actually has negative effects on the immune system, making us more susceptible to disease. See Chapter 2 for a more in-depth discussion of this topic. Second, cortisol increases one's **metabolism** by freeing up glucose stores in the liver, making more energy available for the body to respond to the stressor. In addition, cortisol acts upon the brain to change some physical behaviors. For instance, cortisol suppresses sexual and reproductive behavior, because in times of stress, it is probably more helpful to fight or seek shelter than it is to seek out sex or reproduction.

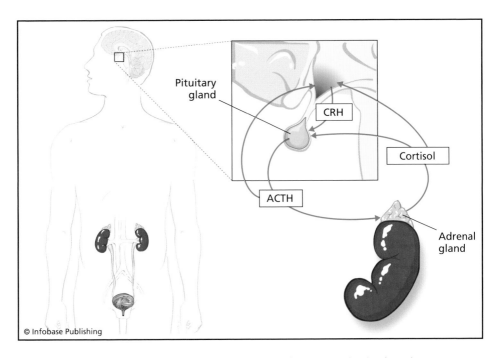

Figure 1.2 The stress response cycle begins when the brain releases corticotrophin-releasing hormone into the pituitary gland (base of brain), which then releases adrenocorticotropin-releasing hormone to signal the adrenal glands (atop the kidneys) to release coritsol into the blood.

These hormonal responses to a single stressful event are not permanent. The brain and pituitary gland are equipped with sensors that detect increased levels of cortisol in the bloodstream and react to it by shutting down CRH and ACTH production, thus decreasing any further cortisol production by the adrenal glands. In other words, the body has its own **negative feedback** system for regulating cortisol production, much the same way gas pump nozzles are equipped with fume sensors that detect increasing levels of gas and shut the pump down when the fumes reach a certain level. This feedback mechanism prevents an overload of cortisol from being produced, because too much cortisol can have a harmful effect on the body (see Chapter 2).

Adrenaline

In addition to the cortisol response, the body responds to stress by producing and releasing **adrenaline** (also called epinephrine) and **noradrenaline** (also called norepinephrine). When a stressor is encountered, the brain rapidly activates the **autonomic nervous system**, the part of the nervous system that controls organs outside the brain and spinal cord (such as the cardiovascular and respiratory systems). The autonomic nervous system uses adrenaline and noradrenaline as its chemical messengers. Within seconds of noticing the stressor, the autonomic nervous system—specifically, the **sympathetic division**—increases heart rate and blood pressure (to get the circulatory system ready for action), increases blood supply to the brain and skeletal muscles (to help us think more clearly and get the muscles ready to act), diverts blood away from the skin and digestive system (these parts of the body are less important during times of stress), decreases stomach acid production (to conserve energy for other parts of the body to use), expands the lungs (to help us breathe better and get more oxygen into the bloodstream), dilates the pupils (to help us see better), causes hair to stand on end (called piloerection), makes the palms sweat (the function of this is unknown), decreases the production of saliva (to conserve energy and fluids), and releases glucose from storage in the liver (to provide energy to the rest of the body). See Figure 1.2 for an illustration of these events. This stress response, also called the **"alarm response"** or **"fight-or-flight response,"** was first described by Hungarian scientist Hans Selye in the 1930s, and is the body's way of preparing the person for reaction to stress.

Someone hiking in the woods who comes across a mountain lion looking as if it is poised to attack would undoubtedly

Figure 1.3 Dr. Hans Selye made important contributions to the study of the human body's reaction to stress. © *Bettmann/CORBIS*

experience stress. CRF, ACTH, and cortisol are released into the bloodstream, along with adrenaline. Heart rate and respiration start to increase oxygen supply to the body's tissues. Blood supply is diverted from the digestive system to arm and leg muscles

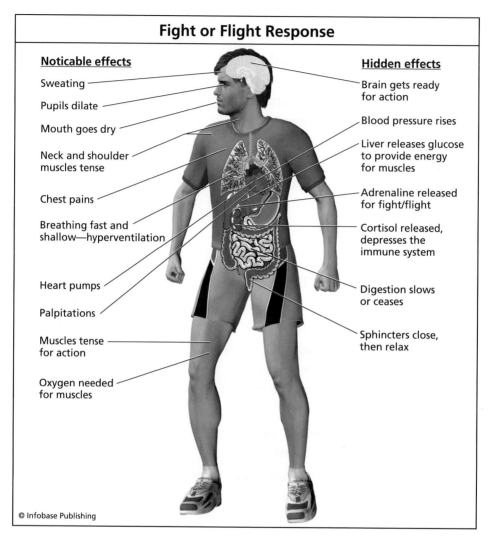

Fight or Flight Response

Noticable effects

Sweating

Pupils dilate

Mouth goes dry

Neck and shoulder
muscles tense

Chest pains

Breathing fast and
shallow—hyperventilation

Heart pumps

Palpitations

Muscles tense
for action

Oxygen needed
for muscles

Hidden effects

Brain gets ready
for action

Blood pressure rises

Liver releases glucose
to provide energy
for muscles

Adrenaline released
for fight/flight

Cortisol released,
depresses the
immune system

Digestion slows
or ceases

Sphincters close,
then relax

© Infobase Publishing

Figure 1.4 Fight or Flight.

to prepare limbs to either engage in combat with the animal
(fight) or flee from it (flight). To help with this, blood vessels
in the skin may start to constrict, causing loss of color in the
face. Glucose is released from glycogen stores in the liver to

supply muscles with energy. Palms start to sweat and the mouth may run dry. Pupils also constrict to reduce excess light from entering the eye and increase visual acuity. The body is now ready to react.

When the stressful event is over, the autonomic nervous system (specifically, the **parasympathetic division**) kicks in, causing the opposite effect to happen: decreasing heart rate and blood pressure, contracting the pupils, producing saliva, and diverting blood flow back to the digestive system. This allows the body to return to its normal state of being. Depending on the

What Stresses You Out?

Despite having their roots in biology, stressors can vary widely from person to person. What stresses one person out does not necessarily do the same to another. Despite individual differences in what people perceive as stressful, stressors generally tend to fall into one of the following categories:

- *critical life changes:* grief over loss of a loved one, care for children or the elderly, birth of a baby
- *daily routine stressors:* finances, legal problems, work, school, communication difficulties, personal health, balancing work/school/family, holiday seasons
- *unrealistic expectations about oneself or others:* misguided sense or responsibility, obsession with personal appearance, interactions with people with mental disorders or substance abuse problems
- *interpersonal relationships:* family relationships, relationships with friends, romantic relationships

nature and intensity of the stressor, however, this return to normal could take hours, days, or even weeks to occur. People often do not recover from stressful events, either psychologically or physiologically, as quickly as they would like.

Health Effects of Chronic Stress

2

There weren't too many things Kevin didn't stress about. He worried about money, grades, his relationships with his parents and friends, what people thought of him—practically everything. Yet there was little basis for his stress. He came from an affluent family, did well in school, had a steady girlfriend, and he got along well with his parents and friends. Kevin was just a worrier. However, by the time he was nearing college graduation, Kevin started to be bothered by some physical illnesses. He became sick with the flu every few weeks, he had a nagging ache in his stomach, and he began to feel depressed all the time. The years of constant stress and worrying had finally caught up with Kevin. He had literally worried himself sick. The constant stress he put on himself had worn down his immune system, given him an ulcer, and caused him to become clinically depressed.

CAUSES OF CHRONIC STRESS

As was discussed in Chapter 1, stress is a normal response to the demands (either physical or psychological) that are placed on us. So, if it is a normal response, stress should be healthy, right? The answer is: sometimes, and sometimes not. There is some evidence that mild amounts of stress can have an overall positive effect. Stress can build character and promote personal growth, psychologically speaking. Medical studies, however, provide more and more evidence that when stress becomes prolonged or chronic, it has negative consequences on the health of the body.

The major causes of chronic stress include being overloaded at school or work, dissatisfaction with one's job, unemployment, uncertainty about the future, isolation from others, divorce, and caring for children. Other external factors that lead to chronic stress are disease, poverty, military combat, and being displaced from one's home. But stress need not be chronic in order to damage physical health; a single tremendously stressful event can cause heart attacks and even miscarriages. Stress can also lead people to make unhealthy lifestyle choices, such as increasing drug and alcohol use and engaging in various criminal behaviors like theft and violence.

There are internal (psychological) factors that can cause chronic stress. People with a so-called **Type A** personality are very intense, competitive, worried, impatient, always in a rush, and show a lot of hostility toward others. In the example at the beginning of the chapter, Kevin exhibited some of the characteristics found in Type A people. Many of the traits exhibited by Type A people can make them more susceptible to the negative health effects of chronic stress. In addition, other **cognitive styles,** or sets of beliefs, make people more prone to chronic stress. These beliefs include a person's perception that he or she cannot control life and the stresses that come along with it, and that stressors occur unpredictably.

STRESS AND SOCIOECONOMIC STATUS

In general, people of lower socioeconomic status are more prone to stress than are those of higher socioeconomic status. Those with a lower socioeconomic status tend to have jobs (often more than one) that involve physical labor, they live in less comfortable conditions, they have poorer educational backgrounds and less social support, and they cannot afford things

Figure 2.1 A woman with her two-month-old son and her family in Garupa, a province of Misiones some 685 miles northeast of Buenos Aires, Argentina, where 65 percent of the people live in poverty and 70 percent of the children are undernourished. © *AP Images*

such as automobiles, babysitters, housing in crime-free neighborhoods, or decent food or health care. In addition, society pays less attention to the needs of people who are lower on the socioeconomic scale. These hardships can bring on a tremendous amount of psychological stress.

Poverty is one of the biggest risk factors for having health problems. Although the stress of a low income does contribute to the health issues that afflict people of lower socioeconomic status, other factors—such as inadequate access to proper health care and inadequate education about healthy lifestyles—can also play a role. In fact, it may be impossible to determine precisely which of these factors contributes most to the conditions (including heart and lung diseases, ulcers, psychiatric disorders, arthritis, and certain types of cancer) that afflict those of lower socioeconomic status.[1,2]

STRESS AND HEART DISEASE

In Chapter 1 it was mentioned that one of the body's immediate physiological responses to stress is increased heart rate and blood pressure. However, when stress levels (and increased cardiovascular system activity) become increased for a prolonged period of time, several things happen. First, the inner walls of the blood vessels begin to wear thin and tear, and as the body tries to repair this damage, the walls of the blood vessels get thicker. Also, the adrenaline released into the bloodstream by stress causes the blood cells that are normally responsible for clotting (called **platelets**) to stick together, making the blood thicken. In addition, chronic stress causes plaques (deposits of fats and other materials) to form in the blood and stick to the vessel walls. This process is called **atherosclerosis**. The plaques eventually make the arteries narrower than normal and can even clog arteries completely. If this happens in one of the blood vessels that supplies the heart with its blood supply, a heart attack can occur. If it happens in one of the arteries that provides blood to the brain, the person may suffer a stroke.

Stress can also cause heart attacks in another way. There are many stories about people having heart attacks in response to a sudden intense stress–such as an earthquake or the sudden loss of a loved one. This happens when the sympathetic division of the nervous system, which stimulates the heart in times of stress, actually overstimulates the heart and causes an electrical surge, called **ventricular fibrillation**. This surge makes the ventricles of the heart contract very quickly and irregularly. The result is that the heart has extreme difficulty restarting its regular beat and cannot pump blood to the body. Ultimately the heart fails, which may cause death. Although ventricular fibrillation tends

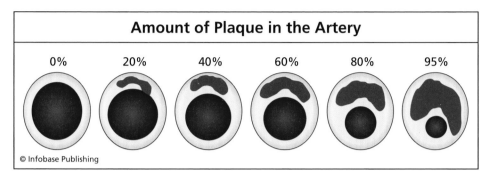

Amount of Plaque in the Artery

0%   20%   40%   60%   80%   95%

© Infobase Publishing

Figure 2.2 Chronic stress can cause plaque to build up in the arteries, leading to constriction of blood flow, and endangering cardiovascular health.

to occur in people who have a history of heart problems (about 75–80 percent of the total number of heart attacks that occur are due to ventricular fibrillation), ventricular fibrillation can also occur in response to extreme stress, even in people without a history of heart disease. For example, on January 17, 1994, a massive earthquake struck the Los Angeles area, causing more than 60 fatalities. An analysis of emergency room records showed that under normal conditions, approximately five people would die daily from heart attacks in the Los Angeles area, but on the day of the earthquake, 24 people died of a heart attack. Of these 24 people, 16 suffered from chest pain or other symptoms within an hour of the initial earthquake.[3]

STRESS AND IMMUNE SYSTEM FUNCTION

A link between stress and the immune system was first demonstrated in the 1940s and 1950s. Physiologist Hans Selye showed that when rats were subjected to mild stress—mild electrical shock or tightly confined environments—over the course of several weeks, the organs involved in producing immune cells, such as the thymus gland (which lies just above the heart), actually shrunk in size. Many subsequent studies in both animals and humans have shown that chronic stress does consistently suppress the immune system. The primary reason stress reduces the activity of the immune system has to do with the stress hormone cortisol. Cortisol inhibits the ability of the thymus gland to produce new immune cells, and can kill off immune cells that are already circulating in the body.

However, the ability of stress to reduce the activity and functioning of the immune system only becomes apparent when the stress is prolonged or chronic. During the first few minutes following the onset of stress, your immune system is actually enhanced, because glands release immune cells into the bloodstream. During the initial rise in blood cortisol levels, cortisol causes immune cells to move out of the bloodstream and into tissues—such as the skin—where they are needed to launch an immune response. Thus, during the onset of stress, the immune system becomes poised and ready for action, but over time, as stress becomes chronic, the strength of the immune system becomes weakened (Figure 2.3).

The ability of stress to alter immune system function has an impact on the body's health. The old saying that stress increases your susceptibility to catching a cold was proven by studies on college students in the 1980s which showed that many more students do become ill with colds during the stress of final exams.[4] By weakening the immune system, stress decreases our ability to fight off viruses that cause colds.

Stress can also have an impact on more serious diseases. It has been shown that stress can weaken our ability to fight off certain types of cancers. A landmark study[5] by Dr. David Spiegel of Stanford University was published in 1989. It showed that women with breast cancer survived longer if they had more social and psychological support. Other studies have shown that after being diagnosed with cancer, people with a positive attitude live longer than those who fall into depression. However,

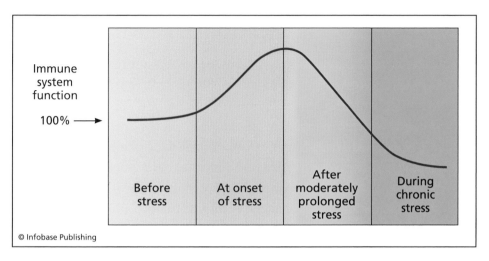

Immune system function

100% →

Before stress

At onset of stress

After moderately prolonged stress

During chronic stress

© Infobase Publishing

Figure 2.3 At the onset of stress, the immune system functions at peak levels. Prolonged stress, on the other hand, diminishes its effectiveness.

the relationship between stress and cancer may not be as simple as it appears. Many other factors–such as lifestyle, diet, type of cancer, age at diagnosis, and type of treatment–influence the way cancer progresses, while other factors–such as access to health care and support groups–influence how people cope with their own cancer.

STRESS AND THE GASTROINTESTINAL SYSTEM

Besides harming the heart and the immune system, stress is also detrimental to the stomach and intestines (also called the **gastrointestinal tract**). In addition to their shrunken thymus glands, the rats that Hans Selye subjected to weeks of stress also developed **ulcers**. The walls of the stomach and intestines are lined with a protective layer of mucous that usually guards these organs against the damaging effects of stomach acid and digestive enzymes. However, small holes in the protective lining can occasionally form, exposing the walls of the stomach or intestines to these harmful substances, resulting in painful ulcers.

It is not known precisely how, or if, stress causes ulcers. Recently, two Australian scientists, Robin Warren and Barry Marshall, won the Nobel Prize in Medicine for their research showing that 90 percent of all stomach ulcers are caused by bacteria called *Helicobacter pylori (H. pylori)*, a strain of bacteria that can infect the mucous lining of the stomach. This research cast doubt on whether psychological factors such as stress can actually cause ulcers. Despite these findings, some researchers still assert that, even though the *H. pylori* bacteria are the main cause of stomach ulcers, it is possible that the ability of stress to suppress the immune system results in a reduced ability to keep these bacteria from eating away at the lining of the stomach and thus assists in the likelihood of developing an ulcer. Other scientists believe that because stress reduces stomach acid secretion, when the stress is over, the body compensates with an acid rebound. Stomach acid is then overproduced and can eat away at the lining of the stomach. Still others believe that since stress diverts blood away from the stomach and intestines, the lack of blood flow can cause small areas of the GI (gastrointestinal) tract to die from lack of oxygen. Finally, others suggest that cortisol suppresses the formation of molecules that promote healing of tissues, including those in the digestive tract. These explanations may account for the 10 percent of ulcers not caused by the *H. pylori* bacterium.

In addition to ulcers, chronic stress may contribute to the development of a disease called **irritable bowel syndrome** (IBS), in which the person suffers from frequent abdominal pain and diarrhea. The precise cause of IBS is not known, and there is a lot of debate as to whether stress plays a role in its development. One thing that is known, however, is that stress can worsen the symptoms of IBS.

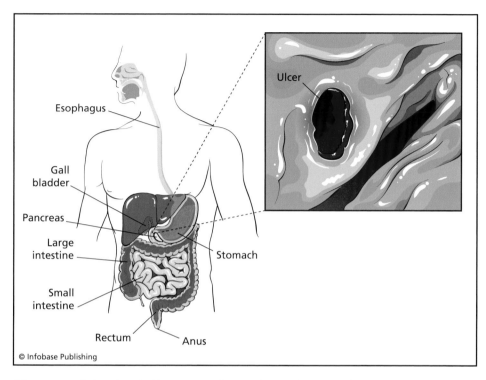

© Infobase Publishing

Figure 2.4 Scientists believe stress is one factor that contributes to or worsens ulcers, which are painful holes in the stomach lining.

STRESS AND MEMORY

Like it does with the immune system, stress has a potentially good and bad relationship with the brain's memory system. In the short term, stress boosts memory. People often remember vivid details about where they were during stressful historic events (such as September 11, 2001, the July 2005 London bombings, and Hurricane Katrina) or stressful personal events (such as being robbed at gunpoint or sexually assaulted). On the other hand, stress can also weaken our memories. The mind may go blank when a person is put on the spot to answer a question in front of the whole class, or during an important exam.

Extreme stress can cause a person to be unable to later remember portions of the stressful time period.

There is a biological basis for the way stress affects memory, either positively or negatively. When people are first faced with a stressor, their sympathetic nervous system increases the heart rate and sends blood from the skin and digestive system toward the muscles and brain instead. This increased supply of oxygen and glucose to the brain makes more energy available to the nerve cells that establish memories. In addition, the increased levels of cortisol in the blood enter the brain and enhance the ability of nerve cells in the **hippocampus** (a brain region that is involved in the formation and retrieval of memories) to encode and store new memories.

However, when stress becomes chronic, cortisol has damaging effects on the hippocampus. Prolonged exposure to high levels of cortisol causes nerve cells in the hippocampus to retract the tiny fibers that they use to make connections with other nerve cells. Some studies have even shown that prolonged elevated levels of cortisol actually cause the hippocampus to shrink in size. Thus, chronic stress can have debilitating effects on memory as well as the underlying brain structures.

STRESS AND DEPRESSION

In the clinical sense, the term **depression** is not meant to describe the occasional feelings a person experiences when he or she is sad. Actual clinical depression is very severe and lasts for weeks, months, or years. People who are clinically depressed feel chronically sad, hopeless, worthless, discouraged, lonely, dejected, guilty, and do not enjoy doing things they used to find enjoyable. People who are depressed often experience disturbances in sleep patterns, fluctuations in weight, lethargy, difficulty concentrating, or decrease in libido. They may even have thoughts of death or suicide.

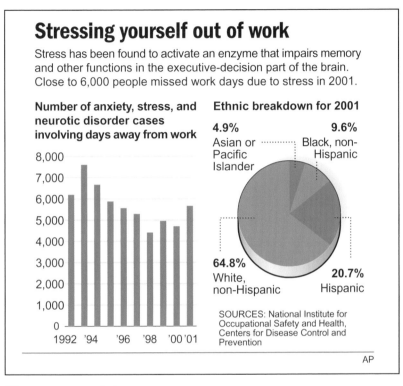

Stressing yourself out of work

Stress has been found to activate an enzyme that impairs memory and other functions in the executive-decision part of the brain. Close to 6,000 people missed work days due to stress in 2001.

Number of anxiety, stress, and neurotic disorder cases involving days away from work

8,000
7,000
6,000
5,000
4,000
3,000
2,000
1,000
0

1992 '94   '96   '98   '00 '01

Ethnic breakdown for 2001

4.9%
Asian or
Pacific
Islander

9.6%
Black, non-Hispanic

64.8%
White,
non-Hispanic

20.7%
Hispanic

SOURCES: National Institute for Occupational Safety and Health, Centers for Disease Control and Prevention

AP

Figure 2.5 © *AP Images*

The link between stress and depression may seem like an obvious one, because people who become depressed are more likely to have major stressors in their life than those who do not. Since it is known that stress increases cortisol levels in the blood and brain, it is not surprising to learn that cortisol also alters the activity of noradrenaline and serotonin, two of the main chemical messengers (neurotransmitters) in the brain that regulate mood. Episodes of depression are quite stressful and cause increased blood levels of cortisol, which may result in a worsening cycle. Depression, while often triggered by psychological problems and stress, may also be caused by a disturbance of the chemistry of brain. That chemical imbalance can often be effectively treated with medications. Since depressed people are more prone to interpret ordinary daily events as stressful, psychotherapy that helps them correct their erroneous thoughts and beliefs is also an important part of treatment.

Since everyone experiences times of stress, it seems curious that some people become depressed while others do not. The reason that different people react differently is unclear, but the answer may be based in either psychology or physiology. For example, psychologically speaking, some people have thought patterns that lead them to perceive regular events as stressful. In other words, they tend to misinterpret the importance of ordinary events. On the other hand, biologically speaking, some people may have a genetic makeup that makes their brains more sensitive to cortisol and the way it changes the activity of chemical messengers such as noradrenaline and serotonin. Today, most scientists believe that depression is the result of an interaction between one's genetic makeup and how he or she reacts to stress.

When Is Stress Life-Threatening?

The detrimental effects of chronic stress on health are usually gradual and evolve over periods of months or years. However, there are times when stress, particularly a very sudden and traumatic stress, can be harmful or even fatal. If you feel any of the following symptoms during a time of stress, call for help immediately:

- heart "flutters" or very rapid heartbeat
- chest pain
- unusual headaches
- thoughts of harming yourself or others

Acute Stress Disorder

3

At 6:55 a.m. on the morning of September 11, 2001, Raymond was still asleep in his Los Angeles home, completely unaware that a major terrorist attack had taken place on the eastern coast of the United States. He was awakened by a phone call from his brother David in New York telling him that one of the World Trade Center towers had collapsed after being struck by an airliner. David's wife Lisa worked on the 65th floor of the World Trade Center, and the two brothers would later find out that she had died in the collapse of the building. They were devastated by their loss. In the few weeks immediately following the attacks, Raymond would often find himself experiencing severe anxiety whenever speaking on the phone with someone. He would also feel like he was outside of his body when he was on the phone, and thought that the person with whom he was speaking sounded like a recording. In addition, almost every night Raymond had nightmares about receiving phone calls to inform him that another member of his family had died in a similar attack. This is an example of what is called acute stress disorder (ASD).

WHAT IS ASD?

Acute stress disorder (ASD) is a psychological disturbance that occurs after observing or being involved in a severely traumatic or horrifying event. The symptoms of ASD are very similar to

Figure 3.1 The south tower of the World Trade Center begins to collapse following the terrorist attacks on the New York landmark, September 11, 2001. © *AP Images*

those observed in people with post-traumatic stress disorder (PTSD, the subject of Chapter 4), except that ASD occurs within the first four weeks after a traumatic event, whereas PTSD occurs over a month or longer following the event.

HOW COMMON IS ASD?

ASD is a newly classified stress disorder that was first defined in 1994 in the 4th edition of the *Diagnostic and Statistical Manual of Mental Disorders* (DSM-IV). As a result of its recent addition to the DSM-IV, information about this disorder is not as readily available as it is for other psychological disorders. Research on ASD is still in its early stages. Most estimates about the prevalence of ASD come from retrospective studies on PTSD. The history of PTSD patients is being examined to determine whether they experienced symptoms during the first four weeks following the traumatic event, which would indicate that they were actually experiencing ASD during this time period.

It is estimated that between 50 and 70 percent of all people will experience some sort of major psychological trauma in their lifetime, whether it be rape, kidnapping, physical assault or other violent crime, military combat or captivity, natural disaster (such as a tornado, earthquake, hurricane, flood, etc.), or terrorism. Major illness and the sudden death of a loved one are also traumatic events that can lead to psychological problems. ASD is more likely to occur when the trauma experienced is a result of malicious intent (like a violent crime) than if it is natural (like a hurricane). For example, survivors of violent crimes have rates of ASD occurrence between 13 and 33 percent, whereas survivors of a typhoon have rates of ASD occurrence of approximately 7 percent.

Of the people who develop ASD after a traumatic event, more than 80 percent go on to develop PTSD within six months if they do not seek psychological help. ASD is often used to predict the occurrence of PTSD, and attempts at intervention and prevention are made during the time the patient is suffering from ASD.

WHO GETS ASD?

Since traumatic events are largely caused by uncontrollable external forces, there is no real genetic or biological basis for ASD. However, factors that contribute to the development of ASD include a person's psychological coping mechanisms and limitations in group or family resources to help deal with the traumatic event. In addition, people who were previously exposed to trauma or have had PTSD in the past are more likely to develop ASD when a new traumatic experience occurs than those who are facing a major trauma for the first time. A person's age, access to psychological support, and factors such as personality, perception and interpretation of the traumatic event, as well as individual expectations, all play a role in the development of ASD.

DIAGNOSIS

Two psychometric methods of evaluation have been developed for the assessment of ASD: the Acute Stress Disorder Interview (ASDI) and the Acute Stress Disorder Scale (ASDS). The ASDI is a specific interview conducted by a psychologist or psychiatrist to determine if a person shows symptoms of ASD. The ASDS is a self-report questionnaire form that a person fills out and gives to a mental health professional who will then evaluate whether the person fits the criteria for being diagnosed with ASD. Both the ASDI and ASDS are based on the official criteria for defining ASD found in DSM-IV as described below. There are seven conditions that are necessary to diagnose a person with ASD:

1. the individual has experienced or witnessed an event that has been threatening to him- or herself or others, and the person's response to the event involves intense feelings of fear, horror, or helplessness;

2. during or after the traumatic event, the person experiences three or more of the following "dissociative" symptoms: (a) a sense of numbing, detachment, or absence of emotional responsiveness; (b) a reduction in awareness of one's surroundings ("being in a daze"); (c) the feeling that one's environment is unreal or dream-like (also called **derealization**); (d) the feeling that one's body is detached or is being seen from the outside (also called **depersonalization**, which is similar to an out-of-body experience); or (e) the inability to remember an important aspect of the traumatic event (also called **dissociative amnesia**);

3. the traumatic event is persistently reexperienced through recurrent images, thoughts, illusions, dreams, flashbacks, or a sense of reliving the event;

4. objects, places, conversations, activities, or people associated with the traumatic event cause emotional distress and are avoided;

5. the person shows symptoms of anxiety and arousal, such as insomnia or difficulty sleeping, inability to concentrate, irritability, increased startle response ("jumpiness"), or restlessness;

6. the disturbance caused by the traumatic event significantly interferes with a person's social, occupational, or academic functioning; also, the symptoms inhibit the person from seeking medical or legal help, or telling other family members about the event; and

7. the disturbance lasts for at least two days but not more than four weeks following the traumatic event.

In addition to these seven criteria for making a diagnosis of ASD, the symptoms described above cannot be the result of taking any medication, another medical condition, or another psychological disorder. Since one of the main criteria for the diagnosis of ASD is the presence of symptoms of anxiety, ASD is considered an anxiety disorder.

The criteria for a diagnosis of ASD are very similar to that for PTSD, and ASD is often considered a precursor for PTSD. However, there are two primary differences between ASD and PTSD. First, ASD occurs only within the first four weeks following a traumatic event, whereas PTSD occurs a month or more after the incident and can last for a longer period of time (months or years). At least 80 percent of people with ASD will go on to develop PTSD. In addition, the diagnostic criteria for ASD focus much more on the **dissociative symptoms** of the disorder, such as derealization, depersonalization, dissociative amnesia, detachment and numbness, and reduced awareness of one's surroundings. These dissociative symptoms are not as severe with PTSD.

Before it became a recognized disorder, ASD was commonly referred to as "shell shock," a military term dating back to World War I in which soldiers would go into a shock-like state after experiencing the trauma of combat. However, it is now apparent that ASD affects both military personnel and civilians.

CASE STUDY

Isabella was a 16-year-old junior in high school. She went to see a psychotherapist after she started to experience a "weird sensation" whenever her boyfriend, Peter, kissed her. She described the sensation as a feeling of floating and staring down at her body from high above. This sensation bothered her so much that she would avoid kissing her boyfriend. Isabella had never experienced this type of feeling before and had not noticed it until a week prior to seeing the therapist. In talking about this sensation with her psychotherapist, Isabella said that she had been recently robbed at knifepoint by a mugger who had surprised her as she was getting into her car in the parking lot of a convenience store. The mugger had held the knife tightly against her throat and demanded the wallet out of her purse. After Isabella had given the mugger her purse, he licked her cheek, leaving saliva on her face.

During psychotherapy, Isabella also told her therapist that, lately, she had also been having nightmares where the mugger was threatening her with the knife. During the day she often had vivid visions of the knife in her mind. Isabella was deeply distressed by these thoughts and nightmares, but she thought she would get over it if she avoided the parking lot where the robbery had taken place. Isabella also avoided cooking in the kitchen at home, since the sight of any knife—even one used for cutting vegetables—made her very anxious and led her to have flashbacks of the mugging. Isabella described herself as very "jumpy," and said that if she was startled by the shutting of a door, her heart would race and it would take several minutes for her come back to normal. Eventually Isabella had to quit her duties as a carpool driver to and from school because she found that she could not concentrate on driving. One day, she even ran a stop sign because she was "out of it." She also had trouble concentrating at school and did poorly on a math exam shortly after the incident.

Isabella's psychotherapist immediately began a type of therapy called cognitive behavioral therapy (CBT). First, she had Isabella join group discussions with other victims of robbery and theft in which the assailant had used a weapon. Here, she was able to explain her experience and compare it with the experiences of other people, and find out how others were dealing with their fear. In addition, Isabella's therapist helped her recognize signs of anxiety (increased heart rate, tightness in the chest, sweating), particularly when she was around things that reminded her of the robbery, such as parking lots and knives. Isabella went through **progressive exposure therapy**, in which her psychotherapist went with her on trips that gradually got closer to the original crime scene. After a while, Isabella was able to go back to the convenience store parking lot, with her psychotherapist along to comfort her and talk her through her feelings.

Although seeing her therapist helped Isabella immensely with her symptoms of ASD, her difficulty sleeping at night and her nightmares continued to bother her. At the recommendation of her therapist, Isabella went to see her family doctor who was able to give her Ambien, a commonly prescribed sleeping pill. The prescription greatly improved her ability to sleep, and the nightmares eventually went away. Isabella never developed any symptoms of PTSD after her traumatic event.

TREATMENT OF ASD

As was mentioned earlier, more than 80 percent of people who experience symptoms of ASD and do not seek psychological help go on to develop PTSD, which can last months or years. Isabella sought treatment soon after her traumatic experience in the robbery and did not go on to suffer from PTSD. Psychological intervention during the first four weeks after the traumatic event can help prevent PTSD from developing. Indeed, it has been estimated that the 80 percent rate at which people with ASD develop PTSD may be reduced to 20 percent with appropriate help and treatment.

To date, the most effective intervention for treating ASD—and perhaps preventing the development of PTSD—is **cognitive behavioral therapy** (CBT). CBT is a type of psychotherapy that is based on the premise that thinking directly affects emotions and behaviors. CBT is designed to change the way a person thinks about the traumatic event that happened to him or her. Through psychotherapy, the person learns to reappraise and reinterpret the event. In addition, patients receive warmth and empathy, help with coping strategies, and opportunities to tell their stories and "talk it out." Therapy is often done in family or group settings with other victims of similar traumas. The sooner the therapy is initiated after the traumatic event, the better the potential outcome. Whenever the ASD sufferer is a child or teenager, group therapy with family or peers is encouraged.

Another goal of CBT is to change a person's behavior in anxiety-provoking situations. Since ASD patients tend to avoid people, places, and objects associated with the traumatic event, they may undergo exposure therapy in which they are brought into contact with such objects and places for increasing lengths of time. This may help desensitize them to the anxiety that those things provoke. In Isabella's case, one aspect of her CBT included visits to the scene of the robbery and other nearby locations, accompanied by her therapist. This exposure therapy helped her deal with her fear of the crime scene, until it was no longer necessary for her to avoid the convenience store where she had been robbed. ASD patients may also be taught anxiety management skills such as **relaxation therapy**, which includes taking deep breaths, mental focusing, meditation, and muscle relaxation techniques.

Another technique used in the treatment of anxiety associated with ASD and PTSD is **biofeedback**. Biofeedback techniques help patients to consciously regulate bodily functions such as

Figure 3.2 A patient undergoes biofeedback monitoring for stress. © *Will and Deni McIntyre/Photo Researchers, Inc.*

heart rate, blood pressure, body temperature, and brain wave patterns. For example, a therapist might attach electrodes to the patient's body to monitor his or her heart rate via an electrocardiograph (EKG), and the readings are displayed on a computer screen that the patient can see. Next the therapist teaches the patient relaxation techniques to help lower their heart rate. The patient is able to monitor the changes in heart rate via the computer screen and observe how well the techniques are succeeding. In order for biofeedback to be effective, patients must spend hours practicing the techniques on their own. Eventually the patient is able to alter their heart rate, blood pressure, or other physiological measures without being hooked up to any sort of biofeedback equipment.

What is Biofeedback?

Biofeedback is a technique in which people are trained to monitor and improve their health by observing their own biological signals. Through the use of technology, biofeedback allows people to see or hear signals put out by their own bodies that they would not ordinarily be able to perceive. An example of a type of equipment that is used in biofeedback is an electrocardiograph, which picks up electrical signals from the heart, amplifies them, and displays them on a computer screen so that the patient may visualize the activity in his or her heart as it occurs. Then, the patient (under the guidance of a doctor or biofeedback specialist) learns to identify events or situations which cause his or her heart to beat too fast. Once the patient can recognize these events (by the sounds or images on the computer screen that indicate the heart is beating faster), the patient is then taught relaxation or other techniques in which he or she becomes able to consciously slow his or her heart rate. With enough proper training, the patient can eventually learn to control his or her heart rate without the use of any equipment at all. The end result is the patient is able to control his or her own physiological responses to stressful events or situations in a way that promotes better health.

Other forms of biofeedback monitor brainwaves, stomach contractions, and activity in skeletal muscles in the arms and legs. Biofeedback is used to treat many maladies including anxiety, pain, headaches, disorders of the digestive system, hypertension, cardiac arrhythmias, and epilepsy. Biofeedback is even used to help paralysis victims relearn to control certain muscles in the body.

If a person is unable to manage the anxiety brought on by the traumatic event through CBT or other forms of psychological therapy, antianxiety drugs such as Xanax, Valium, or Klonopin may be prescribed to reduce anxiety levels to a more manageable level. In addition, antidepressants such as Paxil or Prozac may be prescribed. Sleep aids such as Ambien or Lunesta may also be prescribed for the treatment of the sleeping difficulties associated with ASD.

Post-Traumatic Stress Disorder

On the morning of December 26, 2004, in Thailand, Vineesha watched in horror from her 10th-story hotel room balcony as a huge tidal wave swept across the beach resort where she was staying. She saw dozens of people either smothered by this 25-foot (7.6-m) wave (generated by a magnitude 9.0 earthquake in the Indian Ocean) or picked up and slammed into neighboring buildings. Fortunately for her, Vineesha was safe high above on the 10th floor of her hotel. But today, many months after the Asian tsunami, she cannot go near the ocean or even hear the sound of waves crashing without experiencing horrific flashbacks of what she saw on that day. She feels anxious much of the time, has insomnia mixed with frequent nightmares about drowning, and her performance at work is starting to deteriorate. Even her boyfriend says that Vineesha has trouble expressing her feelings and seems very withdrawn. Vineesha is experiencing post-traumatic stress disorder (PTSD).

WHAT IS PTSD?

Post-traumatic stress disorder, often referred to as PTSD, is a psychological disturbance that occurs after observing or being involved in a severely traumatic or horrifying event. Although most people believe they could carry on with their lives no mat-

Figure 4.1 A Thai hotel employee sits in the lobby of a Patong Beach hotel destroyed by the tsunami of December 26, 2004, one of the worst natural disasters in history. © *AP Images*

ter what may happen to them, some events are so traumatic that people are unable to cope and function after they take place. The symptoms of PTSD are very similar to those seen with acute stress disorder (ASD), which was discussed in Chapter 3. However, the main difference between ASD and PTSD is that symptoms of ASD appear within the first four weeks after the traumatic event, whereas PTSD symptoms appear a month or longer following the event. Often, PTSD symptoms do not appear until six months or more after the trauma.

PTSD is not a new disorder. Descriptions of symptoms that resemble those of PTSD date back to ancient times when humans were attacked by animals or rival tribespeople, or fought in early conflicts such as the Trojan War. Playwright William Shakespeare's character Henry IV (as described by his wife after he returned home from war) shows many of the symptoms of PTSD. During the American Civil War (1861-1865), PTSD was called "Da Costa's syndrome," named after a doctor who wrote about its symptoms. During World War I (1914-1918), it was called "shell shock," and in World War II (1939-1945) it was called "battle fatigue." In the United States, PTSD did not receive a lot of attention from mental health professionals until after the Vietnam War (which the United States stopped fighting in 1973). At that time, studies found that up to 30 percent of Vietnam veterans suffered from symptoms of PTSD. PTSD was first classified as a mental disorder in 1980 by the American Psychiatric Association (APA).

HOW COMMON IS PTSD?

It is estimated that between 50 and 70 percent of all people will experience some sort of major psychological trauma in their lifetime. Up to 20 percent of these people will go on to develop PTSD. This means that as many as 13 million people in the United States alone may have PTSD at any given time. Approximately 8 percent of all adults will develop PTSD, and women are twice as likely as men to develop the disorder (perhaps because women are more often victims of interpersonal violence such as rape and domestic abuse).

Of the people who develop ASD within a month of a traumatic event, more than 80 percent will develop PTSD if they do not seek psychological help to resolve the anxiety and other problems brought on by the event. Because of this, ASD is a very good predictor of PTSD.

WHO GETS PTSD?

Anyone who witnesses or experiences a traumatic event can be susceptible to PTSD. This includes military combat personnel, firefighters and police officers, paramedics, rescue workers, victims of violent crimes, survivors of natural disasters (such as earthquakes, hurricanes, tornadoes, or volcanic eruptions), survivors or witnesses of car or airplane crashes, survivors of political oppression, abused children, and people diagnosed with life-threatening illnesses. Usually, the more intense the trauma, the more likely the person is to develop PTSD. The traumatic event does not have to be associated with a single event, such as a terrorist attack or hurricane. Instead, PTSD can be brought on by prolonged stressful circumstances, such as being abused as a child or tortured for political reasons over a period of months or years.

Not everyone who experiences the same traumatic event develops PTSD. For example, although estimates show that 49 percent of people who are raped go on to develop PTSD, the other 51 percent do not. What makes some people more vulnerable to PTSD than others, even when they all experience the same type of trauma? Researchers have been actively pursuing the answer to this question for several decades, and the answer appears to lie in individual differences between people and their ability to cope with and process major stressful events. There may also be individual biological or genetic factors that contribute to an individual's susceptibility to PTSD. People with little social support, long-lasting childhood traumatic experiences, and those who live in an environment where shame and guilt are associated with a traumatic event (such as in some cultures where being raped or abused as a child places great feelings of shame upon a person and his or her family) also seem to be likely to develop PTSD. In addition, when a traumatic event is perceived as uncontrollable or unpredictable, is sexual in nature, or is perceived with great horror and fear, PTSD is more likely to develop.

DIAGNOSIS

To be diagnosed with PTSD as defined by the American Psychiatric Association (APA), there are six conditions that a person must have:

1. the individual has experienced or witnessed an event that has been threatening to him- or herself or others, and the person's response to the event involves intense feelings of fear, horror, or helplessness;

2. the traumatic experience is persistently reexperienced in one or more of the following ways: unwanted images, memories, thoughts, or perceptions of the event; recurrent dreams about the event; the person acts or feels as if he or she is actually reliving the event and experiences **flashbacks**, which can include hallucinations and illusions of the event taking place again; intense psychological distress is experienced when the person encounters "cues" such as photographs, images, sounds, or symbols that are reminders of the event; and such "cues" also provoke physical responses, such as increased blood pressure or heart rate;

3. the person actively avoids things associated with the traumatic event in three or more of the following ways: the person attempts to avoid thoughts, feelings, or conversations associated with the trauma; the person avoids activities, places, or people that bring up recollections of the trauma; the person has difficulty remembering an important part of the traumatic event; the person shows reduced interest or participation in significant activities in his or her life (such as sports or school); the person feels detached or isolated from others; the person has a diminished ability to express or feel strong emotions such as love or joy; and

the person feels as if his or her future is shortened or
that her or she will not have a career, marriage, children, or normal lifespan;

4. the individual experiences two or more of the following signs of physical disturbance: insomnia, irritability,
difficulty concentrating, or **hypervigilance** (jumpiness
and guarded actions);

5. the symptoms described in points 2, 3, and 4 have lasted
more than a month; and

6. the symptoms result in significant distress or impair-
ment in the person's schoolwork, job functioning, or
family life.

In addition to these criteria, various psychological tests are
used to help mental health professionals determine if a person
has PTSD. Such tests include the Clinician Administered
PTSD Scale (CAPS), the Structured Interview for PTSD (SI-
PTSD), the Anxiety Disorders Interview Schedule (ADIS), the
PSTD Checklist (PCL), and the PTSD Symptom Scale
Interview (PSS-I). These tests are either short questionnaires
that a person fills out and has evaluated by a mental health
professional, or they are interviews (conducted by a trained
psychologist or psychiatrist) that are specifically designed to
determine if a person has PTSD. In addition, physical tests,
such as monitoring the patient's heart rate while he or she is
shown an image related to a specific traumatic event, can also
be used.

PTSD is considered acute if its symptoms at the time of diagnosis have lasted for less than three months. PTSD is considered
chronic if the symptoms have lasted more than three months.
Symptoms of PTSD often immediately follow those of ASD, but
the symptoms can also first appear six months or more after the
traumatic event (this is called delayed onset PTSD).

PTSD is often accompanied by symptoms of other psychological disorders, such as anxiety, panic attacks, or depression. In addition, people with PTSD may engage in self-destructive behaviors such as alcohol or drug abuse, suicide attempts, high-risk sexual activity, or reckless or criminal behavior. PTSD often leads to frequent feelings of anger, problems with family members and interpersonal relationships, decreased libido, and decline in job functioning. Although the symptoms of PTSD can come and go over time, they tend to be particularly intense around times that remind the person of the traumatic event, such as the anniversary of the event (for example, the anniversary of September 11).

People who suffer from PTSD tend to have a number of health problems. Cardiovascular problems such as high blood pressure and heart disease are often seen in PTSD sufferers. Gastrointestinal problems such as ulcers can also accompany PTSD, as can susceptibility to certain types of cancer.

It is often difficult to diagnose PTSD for several reasons. First, PTSD sufferers often think or hope that their symptoms will go away on their own as they "get over" the event that traumatized them. Some people internalize the blame for the traumatic event, thinking they somehow deserve their symptoms. Others believe that their symptoms are too embarrassing or personal to discuss with others, or worry that they will be perceived as weak if they seek counseling. In their efforts to avoid anything that has to do with the event, some sufferers of PTSD do not seek help from mental health professionals because that would mean dealing with the very issues that bother them. In cases where symptoms do not show up until months or years after the traumatic event takes place, PTSD sufferers may not make the connection between a particular event and their feelings of anxiety, anger, and avoidance.

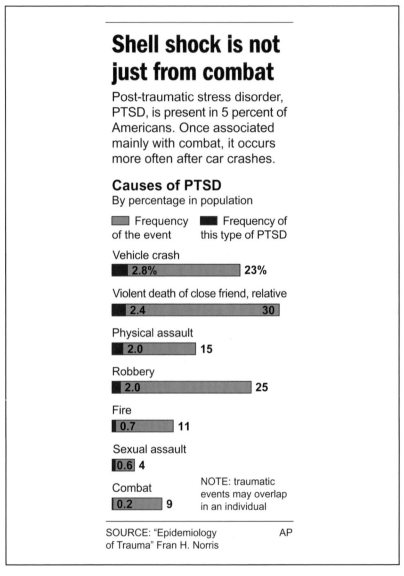

Shell shock is not just from combat

Post-traumatic stress disorder, PTSD, is present in 5 percent of Americans. Once associated mainly with combat, it occurs more often after car crashes.

Causes of PTSD
By percentage in population

■ Frequency of the event   ■ Frequency of this type of PTSD

Vehicle crash
2.8%   23%

Violent death of close friend, relative
2.4   30

Physical assault
2.0   15

Robbery
2.0   25

Fire
0.7   11

Sexual assault
0.6 4

Combat
0.2   9

NOTE: traumatic events may overlap in an individual

SOURCE: "Epidemiology of Trauma" Fran H. Norris   AP

Figure 4.2 © *AP Images*

PTSD IN CHILDREN AND ADOLESCENTS

Children and adolescents are also susceptible to PTSD. Children are prone to develop PTSD if they are the victims of kidnapping or rape, school shootings, car accidents, child abuse, or are a friend or relative of someone who has committed suicide or has been killed. In fact, the rates of PTSD in children and adolescents exposed to trauma are higher than in adults. Also, the younger the child is, the more likely he or she is to develop PTSD. Some 39 percent of preschoolers develop PTSD after a trauma, whereas only 33 percent of middle school students and 27 percent of high school students develop the disorder after the same or similar trauma.

Yet the symptoms of PTSD in children can differ slightly from what is seen in adults. Instead of reexperiencing the traumatic event with feelings of fear, helplessness, or horror, a child might act out and be disruptive to his or her classroom. While an adult might have repetitive and unwanted images of the traumatic event, children often act out a specific portion of the trauma or may incorporate it into their play behavior. For instance, a child who witnesses a shooting may more frequently engage in shooting-type games with other children. Children (especially younger children) who are traumatized may experience a delay in developmental milestones such as toilet training. Adolescents who are exposed to severe trauma are more likely to display impulsive or aggressive behavior.

One factor that influences whether a child or adolescent develops PTSD is how his or her parents react to the traumatic event. Children and adolescents with greater family support and whose parents show less distress over the event are less likely to develop PTSD.

PTSD in children is often treated with forms of play therapy, using drawings or games to help children express their feelings about the event. Cognitive behavioral therapy is also used to explore and correct thoughts such as feeling guilt, shame, or responsibility for the event. Including parents or other family members in the treatment process can be extremely beneficial.

Sarah was an Air Force Master Sergeant who served in the war in Iraq that began in 2003. She was stationed in Kuwait with the 159th Air Refueling Wing of the Air Force Reserve, helping refuel aircraft that conducted bombing raids on Iraq. She never actually saw any combat, and the nearest she came to death was when she helped load planes with the caskets of American and coalition forces that were killed in action. Despite her low-risk assignment, Sarah was deeply affected by her experience. A few months after returning home to New Mexico, Sarah began to feel heart-broken and depressed. She felt as if her heart and mind had been shattered by seeing all these dead soldiers' caskets. She also began to experience mood swings that were sudden and severe. She had to take frequent breaks from her office job and retreat to a restroom to calm down. Sarah had difficulty concentrating at work and as a result she always seemed to be behind in her workload. Sarah also began to cringe every time she heard the sound of an airplane or helicopter passing overhead. Whenever she would hear one, she had visions of running out to the airplane or helicopter and unloading more dead soldiers and placing them into coffins. Sarah knew she had some deeply rooted psychological problems caused by her experiences overseas, but she avoided dealing with her symptoms whenever possible. She began drinking more wine after work, watched TV until late at night, ate and slept less, and became easily irritated. After about 18 months of being back in the United States, her symptoms persisted, and she felt as if her thoughts and feelings weren't going to get any better on their own. Sarah went to the Air Force Reserve recruiting office and asked if they could recommend someone that could help. They referred her to a weekly therapy group held at a nearby psychiatric clinic. Desperate to get rid of her nagging symptoms, Sarah enrolled immediately. The group was made up of 7 other Iraq war veterans who were experiencing similar symptoms of PTSD, and the group was led by Dr. Irving, a psychiatrist who had specialty training in PTSD in military veterans. During the first month of their weekly meetings, the group sat in a circle and each individual was given time to talk about their experiences in the war and the psychological damage it had done to them. Then Dr. Irving began exposure therapy by going on group field trips to shooting ranges, a local military air base, and even out into a nearby desert. On these field trips the PTSD patients would be exposed to the sound of shots being fired, the roar of airplane engines, the chopping sound of helicopters in flight, and the feel of walking on sand, all of which reminded the patients of their experiences in Iraq. While being exposed to these situations, each PTSD patient would be encouraged to talk about feelings or memories that were evoked, and were given emotional support by each other and Dr. Irving. Aside from these field trips, the therapy group was also encouraged to find something they all liked to do and found enjoyable. The group formed their own bowling team, and after each weekly meeting they would go out bowling and enjoy the company of each other. Sarah found comfort in her new friends, especially since they could truly understand her needs as a sufferer of PTSD. Over time Sarah became less anxious whenever she heard the sound of aircraft, and the antidepressant Dr. Irving had prescribed helped relieve her of her feelings of sadness and irritability. She began to eat and sleep better. Although the antidepressant made her feel a bit sluggish at times and she gained a little weight, Sarah felt it was a small price to pay for her escape from the hellish nightmare she had suffered under the grips of PTSD.

TREATMENT OF PTSD

The most effective intervention for treating PTSD is cognitive behavioral therapy (CBT). Through this type of psychotherapy, patients learn to reappraise and reinterpret the event that so drastically affected them. They are taught that since they cannot change the traumatic event that occurred, they can at least change the way they think about it. They also attempt to unlearn the unhealthy emotional reactions they experience when a memory or flashback of the traumatic event pops into their minds. In addition, patients are given warmth and empathy as well as opportunities to tell their stories and "talk it out" (called *psychological debriefing*). The sooner the therapy begins after the traumatic event, the better the potential outcome. Therapy is often done in family or group support settings with other victims of similar traumas, as was described in Sarah's case earlier.

Another goal of CBT is to change a person's behavior in response to anxiety. Since PTSD patients tend to avoid people, places, and objects associated with the traumatic event because it causes anxiety and painful memories, patients may undergo exposure therapy in which they are exposed to such objects and places for increasing lengths of time in order to desensitize them to the anxiety that is brought on by such things. In the case of Sarah, our Iraq war veteran who was troubled by the sound of aircraft, her therapist took her on field trips to a local military airbase, exposing her to these sounds while she was encouraged to talk about the feelings, memories, and anxiety that they evoked. CBT also teaches people how to anticipate and deal with future memories and flashbacks of the event. For example, when Sarah saw an airplane off in the distance before she could

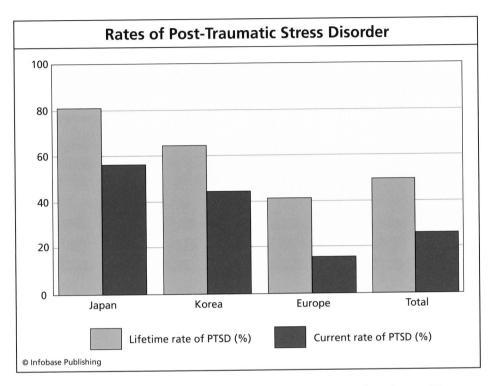

Figure 4.3 Post-Traumatic Stress Disorder incidence among American military service members held as POWs during WWII in Europe, Korea and Japan (Source: Adapted from Engdahl, B., T.N. Dikel, R. Eberly, A. Blank, Jr., "Post-Traumatic stress disorder in a community group of former prisoners of war: a normative response to severe trauma." *American Journal of Psychiatry* 154, no. 11 (1997): 1576-81.)

hear its sound, she learned (with the help of her therapist and support group) how to anticipate and control the anxious feelings that would be brought on by the sound of the airplane once she could hear it.

CBT also provides patients with anxiety management techniques such as relaxation techniques and biofeedback. For example, the military has developed **virtual reality** combat simulators to help war veterans deal with PTSD. Veterans put on goggles and headphones that project images and sounds of battle scenarios. These are designed to provoke anxiety and memories of being in combat, so that the soldiers will be able to recognize and deal with their feelings of anxiety and fear. This type of virtual reality can also be combined with biofeedback measures (such as heart rate and blood pressure monitors) to help veterans learn to control their physiological reactions to stress and anxiety.

Another important aspect of treating PTSD is teaching the use of proper coping skills. One method that researchers have found useful is the process of **active coping**, in which the PTSD sufferer recognizes and accepts the impact that the traumatic event has had on his or her life, and knows that he or she must take direct action to improve things every day. This helps put the PTSD patient in a position of power and control over his or her symptoms, with fewer feelings of helplessness.

Successful treatment of PTSD also requires an understanding of how the recovery process works. People with PTSD should not have unrealistic expectations that they somehow will be instantly cured. Recovery from PTSD is an ongoing, gradual, daily process. The PTSD patient must realize that he or she will probably continue to have painful memories of the event, which may never go away completely. However, successful treatment can result in fewer and less disturbing symptoms and greater confidence in the person's ability to deal with the memories and the emotions they bring.

There are several things a PTSD sufferer should avoid, because they have been shown *not* to help ease the symptoms of the disorder. These include:

• using alcohol or drugs to help reduce anxiety, insomnia, or thinking about the trauma;

- isolating oneself from others;
- reducing participation in activities that were enjoyable prior to the traumatic experience;
- directing one's anger toward others;
- avoiding cues (people, places, or things) that remind one of the event; and
- becoming a "workaholic" to keep busy and avoid the distressing memories.

If a person is unable to manage the anxiety brought on by the traumatic event through CBT or other forms of psychological therapy, anti-anxiety drugs such as Xanax, Valium, or Klonopin may be prescribed to reduce anxiety levels to a more manageable level. In addition, antidepressants such as Paxil, Zoloft, or Prozac may be prescribed, as well as sleep aids such as Ambien or Lunesta for the treatment of the sleeping difficulties associated with PTSD.

MYTHS ABOUT PTSD

Although public awareness of PTSD has grown in recent years, there are still several misconceptions about the disorder. Below are some common myths about PTSD that are known to be false:

1. *PTSD only affects war veterans.* This is false. PTSD can affect anyone.
2. *PTSD is a sign of psychological weakness for those who can't cope and move on with their lives.* False. Trauma often permanently changes the way people view the world and their surroundings. Prolonged trauma over months or years can even alter the chemistry of the

brain. Both of these facts make people susceptible to PTSD, through no fault of their own.

3. *Symptoms of PTSD develop immediately following a traumatic event.* False. Although symptoms of PTSD usually appear within three months of a traumatic event, in some cases, such as in abused children, the symptoms may not begin until much later in life.

Physical Child Abuse 5

A backhand across the face. A kick in the leg. Being shaken violently. Over three-quarters of a million children were abused or neglected in some form or another in the year 2000, according to recent data from the U.S. Department of Health and Human Services. Many maltreated children are more likely to experience learning problems, depression, and stress disorders such as ASD and PTSD. Various stress molecules such as cortisol are often imbalanced in maltreated children and adult survivors. In addition, abused children are often unable to cope with stress and anxiety effectively, and even their biological responses to stress are altered. In fact, extremely stressful situations can cause brain cells to die, resulting in certain brain structures being smaller in adults who were abused as children as compared with those who were not abused.

As discussed in this chapter as well as Chapters 6 and 7, child abuse occurs in several different forms: physical, mental/emotional, sexual, or any combination of these. Whatever the type of abuse a child experiences, the resulting psychological and emotional damage is immense.

HOW COMMON IS PHYSICAL CHILD ABUSE?

Because many cases of child abuse go unreported to police or other authorities, estimates of the prevalence of child abuse vary considerably. Data from the U.S. Department of Health and

Table 5.1 Victims by Age Group and Maltreatment Type, 2004

AGE GROUP	PHYSICAL ABUSE		NEGLECT		MEDICAL NEGLECT		SEXUAL ABUSE	
	Number	%	Number	%	Number	%	Number	%
<1–3	29,733	12.8	169,311	72.9	5,981	2.6	5,145	2.2
4–7	31,389	16.8	119,794	64.0	2,870	1.5	17,018	9.1
8–11	30,793	19.1	96,205	59.8	2,584	1.6	18,294	11.4
12–15	36,089	22.8	85,362	54.0	2,617	1.7	26,133	16.5
16 and older	11,460	24.9	24,098	52.4	713	1.6	7,480	16.3
Unknown/missing	532	22.2	1,462	61.0	26	1.1	278	11.6
Total	**139,996**		**496,232**		**14,791**		**74,348**	
Percent		**17.8**		**63.0**		**1.9**		**9.4**

AGE GROUP	PSYCHOLOGICAL ABUSE		OTHER ABUSE		UNKNOWN		TOTAL	
	Number	%	Number	%	Number	%	Number	%
<1–3	11,067	4.8	37,673	16.2	653	0.3	259,463	111.8
4–7	11,954	6.4	27,377	14.6	497	0.3	210,899	112.7
8–11	11,881	7.4	23,617	14.7	365	0.2	183,739	114.2
12–15	10,716	6.8	22,222	14.1	424	0.3	183,563	116.2
16 and older	2,871	6.2	6,689	14.6	136	0.3	53,447	116.3
Unknown/missing	207	8.6	76	3.2	5	0.2	2,586	107.9
Total	**48,696**		**117,654**		**2,080**		**893,797**	
Percent		**6.2**		**14.9**		**0.3**		**113.5***

Data Source Child File.
Based on data from 45 states.
*Total percentage exceeds 100 percent due to overlap among categories.

Human Services found that in 2004,[7] almost 800,000 children were found to be victims of abuse or neglect. About 18 percent of these were cases of physical child abuse.

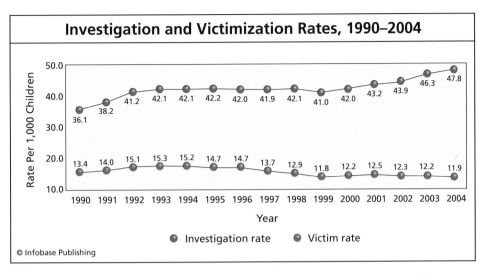

Figure 5.2 Child Abuse Investigation and Victimization Rates, 1990-2004

DEFINITION OF PHYSICAL CHILD ABUSE

Defining physical child abuse is a complex issue. What makes it so complicated is the fact that there are many legal and cultural differences about what is considered physical abuse and what is not. For example, spanking a child for misbehavior is not considered physical abuse in most parts of the world. Some cultures condone physical punishment of children, even if the punishment is somewhat severe (such as hitting a child's feet with a piece of wood until the child can no longer walk). Other cultures do not tolerate inflicting any sort of pain upon children. In the United States, it is generally believed that mild physical punishment, such as spanking, is not child abuse, mainly because it does not cause significant physical injury. However, more severe punishment, such as beating a child until he or she has bruises or broken bones, is considered physical abuse in our society. Today in the United States, psychologists, social workers, and the judicial system generally define physical child abuse as the nonaccidental injury of a child inflicted by a parent or caregiver (such as a grandparent, foster parent, legal guardian, babysitter, or nanny).

CAUSES OF PHYSICAL CHILD ABUSE

There is no single factor that leads to the physical abuse of a child. The most common reason people believe children are physically abused is that the parent or caregiver has personality, anger, or stress management problems. Parents who are overwhelmed with stress from work or family problems may direct their frustrations toward their children and end up physically abusing them. For example, a single mother working two jobs to provide for her three-year-old son and infant daughter might become so distraught when the baby wakes up hungry repeatedly throughout the night that she shakes her baby severely in an attempt to make her stop crying.

Another factor that leads to physical child abuse is the interrelationship between the caregiver and the abused child. For example, if a parent views his or her child as difficult and becomes stressed by the child's defiant behavior, the parent may lash out and strike the child. This, in turn, can make the child more resentful of the parent and subsequently more defiant. This cycle of misbehavior, abuse, and further misbehavior is known as an **interactional process**. In other words, there is an interaction between the child's behavior and the parent's reaction that contributes to the abusive situation.

Other factors also influence physical child abuse. For example, people living in poverty often experience more life stressors than those in financially stable conditions, and this increased stress can lead to a greater probability of physically abusing a child. However, physical child abuse can occur in all socioeconomic classes of society, even in the wealthiest of families. Children with physical or mental handicaps can also be at increased risk for physical abuse, due to the parent's increased stress from having to care for the handicapped child (for example, one who is confined to a wheelchair or cannot feed him- or herself). Children with behavioral problems such as attention-deficit/hyperactivity disorder (ADHD), which can cause increased misbehavior as well as increased stress on the parent (this is another example of an interactional process) are at increased risk for being physically abused. Other factors include the presence of domestic violence. A husband who physically abuses his wife is more likely to physically abuse his children as well. The age of a child also seems to be a risk factor for physical child abuse: According to 2004 statistics from the U.S. Department of Health and Human Services,[7] children age three or younger experienced the highest rate of abuse. This is likely due to the fact that young children are the most vulnerable and defenseless, and because their behavior (not knowing right from wrong, crying throughout the night) is more likely to put increased stress on a parent than the behavior of older children.

SIGNS THAT A CHILD IS BEING PHYSICALLY ABUSED

There are some telltale signs that a child is being physically abused. The first is the presence of bruises. Although bruises can occur as a result of accidental falls, bruises in an infant who cannot yet walk are especially suspicious. Also, bruises in certain places, such as the back of the legs, upper arms, torso, or neck or head (where bruises from playing or falling are less likely to occur) and bruises with a particular imprint (such as in the shape of an adult bite mark or handprint) are also likely to be a result of physical abuse.

Broken bones—although less common than bruises—are also indicators of child abuse (especially when the child is not yet walking, and therefore not suffering accidental falls). Bone fractures of abused children are usually seen in the arms and legs, ribs, or skull. Other injuries, such as ruptured internal organs,

Figure 5.3 A social worker questions a little boy about his broken arm as she seeks out possible child abuse. © *Steve Kagan/Time Life Pictures/Getty Images*

are also sometimes seen in abused children. Blows to the head can also cause **subdural hematomas**—small hemorrhages on the surface of the brain. Sometimes, physically abused children are intentionally burned by cigarettes, stovetops, or boiling water.

Recently, the media have given a lot of attention to what is termed **shaken baby syndrome**, which is responsible for about half of all nonaccidental deaths of children. When a parent or caregiver violently shakes a small infant or child in anger, damage to the head and brain can occur more easily because the child's neck muscles are not yet fully developed. The result can be brain damage and bleeding, detached retinas, nerve damage, and even death.

PSYCHOLOGICAL EFFECTS OF PHYSICAL ABUSE
Because they have not fully developed their language skills, infants and young toddlers usually cannot tell anyone that they are being physically abused, but there are some behaviors that may indicate he or she is being abused. Some abused infants develop a shrill, unique cry that other babies do not emit. Abused infants often show apprehension when they hear other children cry. Abused children do not seek comfort from their parents as normal children do, and they sometimes show a decreased interest in playing with toys.

A slightly older child (ages 2 through 4) who is physically abused may have frequent temper tantrums and may have trouble with developmental milestones such as toilet training. As the abused child enters preschool or kindergarten, learning problems and low self-esteem tend to show up as poor performance in school. Abused children often tend to withdraw from other children and do not socialize normally. They may also become hypervigilant (overly watchful). In addition, since children often learn by example, a physically abused child who becomes angry over something may show physical aggression toward other children, animals, or adults.

When abused children are of elementary school age and are more mentally advanced than younger children, other behavioral signs of abuse can surface. These may include an increased desire for control over how their toys are organized (because children have no control over being abused), adaptation to the abuse pattern (for example, intentionally falling asleep early before the father gets home from work to avoid any potential abuse), reduced talking (since talking can sometimes get them into trouble at home), fear of failure, difficulty following instructions, and regression (for instance, a seven-year-old may wet the bed or his or her pants even if he or she has been toilet-trained for years).

As adults, victims of physical child abuse often have difficulty trusting other people and committing to relationships. They feel a great deal of anger about the past abuse and may direct this anger outward (resulting in aggression toward others) or inward (leading to depression or self-destructive behavior).

PHYSICAL ABUSE OF ADOLESCENTS

For a long time, the problem of physical abuse of adolescents (teenagers) was overlooked. It was commonly believed that teens were less vulnerable because of their almost-adult size and strength. In addition, it was thought that adolescents could effectively avoid abuse by running away, protecting themselves, or getting help. However, physical abuse of adolescents remains a significant problem in society today.

It is rare for a parent to start abusing their children when they are adolescents; normally, abused teenagers have been abused as children as well. Teens who are abused often turn to drugs or alcohol to dull their pain and/or ignore or deny their abuse. Occasionally, abused teenagers will intentionally provoke abuse from their parents in an attempt to achieve some degree of control over the situation. Abused teens tend to be more aggressive than others their age both physically and verbally. As with abused children, social withdrawal, low self-esteem, and depression are often seen in abused adolescents.

CHARACTERISTICS OF ABUSIVE PARENTS OR CAREGIVERS
In general, parents or caregivers who physically abuse their children have anger and stress management problems and lack the ability to cope with the responsibilities of being a parent, or lack

Munchausen Syndrome by Proxy

One very interesting psychological syndrome that results in physical abuse of a child is referred to as Munchausen syndrome by proxy. This syndrome has been depicted in popular movies, novels, and television shows. In adult Munchausen syndrome, the adult intentionally fakes an illness or harms him- or herself to receive attention from family members or medical care personnel. It is believed that people with adult Munchausen syndrome engage in self-destructive behavior out of anger toward their own parents for making them feel abandoned, or that these people have developed pathological means to satisfy their need for attention. In Munchausen syndrome by proxy, however, the adult (almost always the mother) intentionally harms her child in order to receive attention from family members or medical staff. Most often, the abuse comes in the form of giving the child excessive amounts of medication or substances that make the child sick. Some cases of Munchausen syndrome by proxy have even resulted in death and can be mistaken for sudden infant death syndrome (SIDS), the sudden, unexplained death of an infant.

appropriate outlets to vent their frustrations about parenting or other life stressors. Characteristics commonly found in abusive parents include low self-esteem, the feeling that their needs are not being met, an inability to separate feelings of anger and frustration from their actions, an excessive need for instant gratification, an inability to accept responsibility for their own actions, and a tendency to blame their faults on others. Parents with personality disorders, depression, or substance or alcohol abuse, or those who are in relationships with domestic violence are also more likely to become abusive. Many abusive parents have had dysfunctional childhoods of their own.

ABUSE BY SIBLINGS

Parents and caregivers (such as legal guardians, grandparents, babysitters, and nannies) are not the only ones who physically abuse children. A child's own sibling, such as an older brother or sister, can also be the abuser. Some estimates indicate that physical abuse by a sibling may actually be more frequent than by a parent. Although it is common for brothers and sisters to fight over disagreements and physically hit, slap, kick, or bite one another, in some cases the violence can escalate into life-threatening situations that involve choking, suffocating, or using a weapon such as a gun or a knife. Sibling abuse is more common in boys who abuse their younger brothers, and tends to happen in households where domestic violence occurs, since the child learns the practice of physical abuse by watching the physical altercations between his or her parents.

INTERVENTION AND TREATMENT

The first step toward ending a particular case of physical child abuse is intervention. Usually, abused children or their siblings are unable to report their abusive parents themselves for fear of the severe repercussions that might follow. Most commonly, the people who end up reporting cases of child abuse are outside family members (aunts, uncles, or grandparents), teachers, emergency room doctors or nurses, pediatricians, or parents of the children who are friends with the abuse victim. Reports are usually made to the police, who refer the case to a government agency that deals with child abuse. In the United States, this agency is called Child Protective Services (CPS). Once an alleged abuse is reported, CPS assigns a social worker to the case. The government agency then investigates the case by interviewing the parents, the child, the child's friends, and teachers. If the government agency feels the allegations of child abuse might be true, then the legal system may get involved and a court order can be issued to remove the child from the home for temporary placement in the care of relatives or foster parents. If there is sufficient evidence for abuse, the abusive parent can be arrested, jailed, and prosecuted. If the abuser is convicted and loses custodial rights, the child can be permanently placed with relatives, foster parents, or put up for adoption.

Treating the victims of physical child abuse is often a difficult task. It is not just the child who must be treated; the abusive parents need treatment as well. Often, the abusive parents are resistant to treatment, since they view the issue as a family matter. The main goal of treating the abusive parent is to get him or her to stop battering the child. This often requires the physical removal of the child from the home while the parent undergoes counseling. Through psychological and behavioral therapy, the parent learns to identify and recognize the feelings, events, and signals that lead to abuse. In addition, abusive parents must learn different ways to cope with anger and stress. They must also learn about child development and what to expect of their child at a particular age (for example, if the parent strikes the child when he or she soils his diapers, then the parent must learn more about toilet training and the ages at which it occurs normally). Abusive parents are also taught to improve communication with their children and to appreciate their children as independent human beings.

Treatment of the physically abused child is also difficult and complex. After medical care is given to treat the physical wounds, intense and lengthy psychological therapy is often needed. At first, the child may resist treatment because he or she is fearful and wary of outsiders and distrustful of adults. The child may also suffer from delays in development and show regression to earlier stages of development. For example, the child may need to be retrained to use the toilet. In addition, there are likely to be behavioral issues (such as aggressiveness and impulsivity) that need to be addressed. The child may need to learn skills to manage anger appropriately. Also, because low self-esteem is very common in physical child abuse victims, confidence-building is a key goal of treatment. In very young children who have limited communication skills, play therapy is often used to help the child express him- or herself and learn self-confidence. Since abused children often become withdrawn, socialization skills may also need to be taught.

CASE STUDY

One of the best portrayals of an abused child can be found in the 1997 movie *Good Will Hunting*. In this movie, the main character, Will (played by Matt Damon), is an orphan who was physically abused by his foster parents. While he is working as a janitor at a university, Will's exceptional intelligence is noticed by a mathematics professor who catches Will solving complex math problems posted outside a college classroom. Despite his intellectual genius, Will is extremely misguided and has no career ambitions at all. The professor eventually gets Will to go see a psychologist named Dr. Sean

McGuire (played by Robin Williams), who repeatedly attempts to get Will to open up. Will eventually meets and starts dating a college student named Skylar (played by Minnie Driver). Through her conversations with Will, the audience learns that Will had an extremely dysfunctional childhood and was beaten by his foster parents, who put out cigarettes on his skin.

Will displays many of the characteristics of a physical child abuse victim. He is defiant of authority, does not trust other people, has a long criminal history, resists opening up about his feelings, lies about his family, cannot commit to an intimate relationship, has low self-esteem and few life ambitions, and seems to drift from one job to the next. During psychotherapy, Will at first refuses to show his true feelings, but in one of his final counseling sessions, he breaks down crying after Dr. McGuire hones in on Will's abusive past and tells him, "It's not your fault."

Although, in the movie, Will does not receive extensive psychological treatment to help him deal with his abusive childhood and his emotional and behavioral issues, speculation can be made as to what a therapist might focus on in treatment with Will. First, a therapist would have to work on Will's trust issues to get him to trust others again (including authority figures). Also, Will would need to work on communication issues and his inability to open up to people, especially if he is going to have a long-term relationship with Skylar. A therapist would also help Will learn to channel his anger into more appropriate outlets, rather than picking fights. Finally, a therapist might help Will improve his self-esteem so that he has a better sense of self-worth and will be able to make his intellectual gifts work for him, both personally and professionally.

MYTHS ABOUT PHYSICAL CHILD ABUSE

There are several commonly held beliefs about physical child abuse that are not always true. The first is that children who are physically abused grow up to become parents who physically abuse their own children. Although many adults who physically abuse their children were themselves abused in their youth, this does not automatically mean that a child who is abused will grow up to be an abuser. Intervention to stop the pattern of abuse, combined with psychotherapy and healing for the abused person, can often change the way someone views violence and can result in that person becoming a healthy and happy parent.

A second common myth about physical child abuse is that the abused child will end up as a drug user, prostitute, or criminal. In fact, many victims of child abuse do *not* turn to illegal behavior as teens or adults. In addition, some criminals, drug addicts, and prostitutes were not abused as children. Although anger from child abuse often results in misbehavior, different people channel anger in different ways, so not all physically abused children become criminals or misfits in society.

One final myth about physical abuse is that once a child is abused, the damage is irreparable. With psychological and family help, survivors of child abuse can learn to not live in the past or blame themselves for being victims. They can also come to realize that, although they cannot change the past, they can take control of their lives and change their future for the best.

Mental Child Abuse and Neglect

6

Randi had no anger problems until after her divorce from her husband Steve. When Steve left her for another woman, the ensuing divorce was lengthy and emotionally painful. While Randi was able to keep custody of her 6-year-old son Taylor, she was forced to move out of her spacious house in the suburbs of San Francisco, and had to take a job to pay the bills and rent for her small apartment. Randi harbored a lot of bitterness toward Steve, and became very stressed because of her tight budget and lack of help to raise Taylor. Eventually she began to direct a lot of her anger toward Taylor. When Taylor would misbehave at home, Randi would shout things like "I wish you were never born!" and "Why can't you be a normal kid?" One time after Taylor spilled food at the dinner table, Randi shouted, "That was a stupid thing to do! Why are you so stupid?!?"

Comments like these can leave deep psychological scars on a child when they are made by a parent or other caregiver. These scars can sometimes be even worse than those that happen through physical abuse. Physical wounds heal, but psychological wounds can last for years. Even greater damage can be done when the child's very existence is not acknowledged–not even his or her need for food. This chapter will explore both mental child abuse (also called **psychological maltreatment**) and neglect. Both of these forms of abuse can be enormously stressful to the child and cause severe psychological damage, often leading to

Figure 6.1 This illustration of a scene from Charles Dickens' novel *Oliver Twist* depicts the neglectful treatment children often received from institutions and orphanages in the past. © *Bettmann/CORBIS*

mental and behavioral problems in the child that continue well into adulthood. Although mental child abuse and neglect are not as likely to result in stress disorders such as ASD and PTSD, the consequences are equally as distressing and devastating.

DEFINITIONS OF PSYCHOLOGICAL MALTREATMENT AND NEGLECT

There are many terms used to refer to psychological maltreatment or abuse of children. Some call it "emotional, psychological or verbal abuse," while others call it "mental cruelty." Regardless of the terms used, psychological maltreatment is not a single event in which a parent verbally assaults his or her child. Rather, it is a continuing pattern of parental behavior that is psychologically destructive to the child. Usually, it includes several of the following: *rejection* (the parent refuses to acknowledge the child's needs and sense of self-worth), *terrorization* (the parent verbally assaults the child or bullies/frightens the child), *isolation* (the parent keeps the child from making friends and having normal social experiences), or *corruption* (the parent encourages the child to engage in inappropriate or illegal behavior).

Another part of psychological maltreatment in a child can be *neglect*, where children are ignored or left alone so much that their well-being is endangered. Neglect can be *physical* (a child is not given proper food or clothing), *medical* (a child is not given medical treatment when needed), *educational* (a child is allowed to skip school, is not even enrolled in school at all, or is not taught proper communication skills), *motor* (a child is not given toys or puzzles to play with to develop fine motor skills), or *emotional* (the child is not encouraged or permitted to form a loving bond with a parent). When compared to other forms of child abuse (physical or sexual), neglect is unique in that the damage is done not by what a parent intentionally *does* to the child, but rather what he or she does *not* do.

CAUSES OF PSYCHOLOGICAL MALTREATMENT AND NEGLECT

Parents who psychologically mistreat their children usually believe that parenting is a tiresome, frustrating job that does not bring them the respect they deserve. Feeling unrewarded for their efforts, parents may take out their frustrations on their children by belittling or insulting them. In addition, parents who psychologically abuse their children are often narcissistic (self-absorbed) and feel that raising children gets in the way of their own lives and the things they would rather be doing.

Families in which psychological maltreatment occurs are usually dysfunctional in some way and lack good communication skills. For example, the children of alcoholics or drug addicts are often psychologically damaged by their parents' substance abuse and the attention it takes away from them. Factors such as parental divorce or separation, poverty, and unemployment can also cause a parent to direct their inability to cope with stressors toward the children. When a child is the result of an unwanted pregnancy, one or both of the parents often vent their frustrations toward the child. In this case, the parents may see their child as an inconvenience and do not want the responsibilities of the unwanted status of parenthood.

The most common cause of child neglect is poverty. However, growing up in a poor environment does not necessarily mean that the child will be neglected. Many other factors, including the efforts and attitudes of the parents, their ability to maintain a steady income, and their inability or unwillingness to obtain government assistance (welfare) can also contribute to neglect. Despite poverty being a major contributor, neglect often occurs in middle class and wealthy families as well.

Neglect doesn't just happen to one child–all the children in a given family are usually neglected. The prevalence of child neglect is highest among children who are less able to care for themselves, usually age three or younger. A 2000 survey[8] found that of the approximately 1,100 children who died in the United States from maltreatment in 1998, more than 50 percent were neglected.

Although it is hard to believe that a parent would not instinctively know how to feed his or her child and give the child the most basic necessities, people who grow up in extremely impoverished or dysfunctional environments may not know any better. Having grown up in an unhealthy environment, it is likely that they never learned how to care for a child properly.

Neglectful parents are often isolated, lack social support or friends, and do not have proper judgment about how to care for their children. They may also be indifferent to the needs of their children. Mental illness, marital problems, and substance abuse are also common among neglectful parents.

SIGNS OF MALTREATMENT OR NEGLECT

Psychologically abused children, as a result of being belittled and insulted by their parents for years, often have low self-esteem and self-confidence and feel inadequate, unloved, and unwanted. As a result, children may respond to the abuse by directing their negative feelings about themselves inward and becoming depressed, suicidal, or withdrawn. Abused children may also turn to self-destructive behaviors such as drug or alcohol use, crime, or skipping school. They tend to be psychologically fragile and need constant reassurance. Alternatively, children may react to psychological abuse by directing their negative feelings outward, behaving aggressively toward others. Psychologically abused children often tend to be attention grabbers, acting out or dressing in unusual clothing to get the attention from outside sources that their parents failed to give them. By the time they are adolescents, the emotional and behavioral problems that these children exhibit can become fixtures of their personality.

Child neglect often involves malnourishment and a failure to provide children with enough food, and there are some obvious signs of neglect that a medical professional should be able to detect. One such medical syndrome is called **nonorganic failure to thrive** (NFTT). In these cases, an infant's weight falls within the lowest 5 percent of all babies his or her age. Malnourishment can also cause slightly older children to develop **psychosocial dwarfism** (PSD), a condition in which the child fails to grow at a normal rate. In both of these syndromes, the children are underfed and may have a host of other medical or behavioral problems such as extreme fatigue, poor muscle tone, and eating problems.

If neglected children survive malnourishment, by the time they reach preschool other symptoms may emerge. Their motor and language skills may be delayed in developing and they may have a distended (expanded or bloated) stomach and very skinny arms and legs. Poor skin tone due to a lack of nutrients may also be present, as well as head lice (which may result from a lack of hair cleaning). Infectious diseases such as tetanus and diphtheria may afflict neglected children, because their parents often fail to keep their immunizations current.

Psychologically, neglected children often have difficulty expressing their emotions because of the lack of emotional stimulation they receive at home. Neglected children often end

A Horrible Experiment

It has been reported that a horrible experiment was conducted in the 13th century by the Emperor of Germany Frederick II. In 1211, Frederick II wished to discover the natural "language of God," the language that is innate to all human beings. He therefore had dozens of children raised in complete silence, with no language taught to them at any time, hoping that this "language of God" would then emerge after their silence was broken. However, no language ever emerged— the children were never able to speak and all of them died in childhood.[9] Today, most developmental psychologists would agree that all language is indeed learned, though our *ability* to learn it is likely rooted in biology. Fortunately, modern science eliminates the need for any such deplorable experiments on children.

up having language development and communication problems, as well as difficulty socializing. Also, children who were subject to neglect may not have had consistent feeding schedules or knew what to expect in terms of care on a day-to-day basis, so they often expect instant gratification when it comes to the things they want.

INTERVENTION AND TREATMENT

It is often very difficult for authorities to intervene in cases of psychological maltreatment of children. In the United States, in order for Child Protective Services to step in when there is a case of psychological maltreatment, it must legally be demonstrated that there is identifiable parental misbehavior, harm to the child, and a link between these two phenomena. However, emotional abuse is not easy to prove or document, especially when there are no real physical signs of abuse. Most abusive parents are self-absorbed and react with great hostility to criticism, denying that any form of abuse is taking place. As a result, they may be reluctant to cooperate with authorities who are investigating reports of abuse.

Similar resistance to intervention is observed in neglectful families. However, because of the malnourishment and physical danger to the child's health, authorities often have more legal leverage to intervene, even if the parents object. Once a social worker or other intervention authority is able to gain the trust of the neglectful parent, he or she tries to help provide access to food, medical services, clothing, and other necessities for the children. In addition, the social worker might try to provide some sort of counseling and education about the physical, emotional, and nutritional needs of children. In some cases, when the home environment remains unsatisfactory, the children are removed and placed into protective custody or foster homes.

EXAMPLES OF PSYCHOLOGICAL MALTREATMENT

Trevor's father was a skilled neurosurgeon and his mother a trial lawyer. Both of them were extremely focused on having successful careers. Trevor, his parents, and his little sister, Beth, lived in a spacious penthouse in Manhattan. Because both of their parents worked, Trevor and Beth attended after-school day care until their mother picked them up after work. Although Trevor's parents were mild-mannered and never hit their children, they were very self-absorbed and paid little attention to the emotional needs of Trevor and Beth. Trevor's father worked long hours. By the time he got home from work, he was too tired to pay much attention to his children and was often glued to the television. Trevor's mother, on the other hand, often took the frustrations of her work out on her children. When she was stressed out over a trial at work, she often felt like her children were getting in the way of her professional life. She would often explode at them for trivial things, such as leaving toys around the house, shouting things like, "You don't even deserve to have these!"

One time, both Trevor and Beth came home from school with mediocre report cards. Upon seeing them, their mother tore them up and shouted, "This is despicable! Your father and I never had grades like this!" Her words drove both children to tears. They ran to their father, but he was distracted watching a basketball game on television. When their father later found the torn-up report cards on the kitchen counter, he asked his wife about them and she lied, saying that she had torn them up by accident because she thought they were junk mail. When Trevor and Beth finally stopped crying, their mother told them they were being too sensitive and should "grow up."

Years of this kind of emotional abuse took its toll on the two children. When Trevor entered middle school, he began to become delinquent from school because he thought education was a waste of time. He started to hang out with some friends who were into drugs, and he often smoked marijuana when he skipped class. Beth, on the other hand, reacted quite differently to the psychological mistreatment she received at home. She had little self-esteem and very few friends. She wasn't very good at making friends because she feared being rejected. When she was in the 5th grade, she started taking scissors and cutting herself on the forearms and legs. She would even try to make little patterns out of the cuts so that she could continue to look at her injuries after they turned to scabs. Once, Beth's teacher caught her doing this and whisked her away to the school nurse. After the nurse put bandages on her cuts, Beth liked the nurse immediately and didn't want to leave. She loved the caring attention the nurse gave her, something she never got from her mother.

Both Trevor and Beth were eventually sent to the school counselor, who referred them to a psychologist who worked with abused children. They were both reluctant to go at first, but after persuasion by school officials, they began to have weekly visits with the psychologist during recess at school. During their sessions, both children recalled the instances of psychological abuse they had experienced with their parents for years. Suspicious, the psychologist called Child Protective Services to investigate. A social worker was assigned to the case and interviewed both Trevor and Beth and their parents. Although the children both gave accurate accounts of the types of emotional abuse they received, their parents completely denied any wrongdoing and later punished their children for making up stories. Without any real proof of psychological abuse, the social worker could not intervene, and the case had to be dropped.

AN EXAMPLE OF NEGLECT

Deanna was a sophomore in high school when she and her boyfriend became sexually active, and Deanna became pregnant.

Deanna had been physically abused as a child, and had run away from home at the age of 16 and moved into a run-down apartment on the south side of Boston. When she realized she was pregnant, Deanna dropped out of high school and took a job as a waitress in a diner to pay the rent and living expenses.

About a month before Deanna was due to give birth, her boyfriend became overwhelmed by the impending responsibilities of parenthood and left Deanna for another girl. Although she was devastated, Deanna carried the baby to term and gave birth to a healthy baby boy, Connor, at the county hospital. Both Deanna and her baby were discharged from the hospital, and Deanna felt there was nothing she could do but try to raise Connor by herself in her run-down apartment.

About two weeks after she gave birth to Connor, Deanna fell into a deep **postpartum depression** (a type of depression that approximately 10 percent of women experience soon after giving birth to a child; postpartum depression is believed to be a result of hormonal changes that occur after the child is born). She was so depressed that she had frequent thoughts of suicide. Often, she could not muster up enough energy to get out of bed. When Connor would wake up crying in the middle of the night because he was hungry or had a dirty diaper, Deanna would just roll over and cover her ears, thinking, "What's the use? He can wait until morning." Eventually, Connor stopped gaining weight and became lethargic. Deanna started to put a bottle of baby formula (watered down, since it cost nearly $20 for a week's supply) in the crib next to Connor at night so she wouldn't have to get out of bed to feed him, but Connor was too weak to lift the bottle and feed himself. So, he would lie there every night, hungry and wearing nothing but a soiled diaper.

Fortunately, the landlord's apartment was directly above Deanna's. The landlord had become increasingly concerned over the sound of Connor's constant crying and the smell of feces wafting through the ventilation system. One day, he made an unannounced visit to Deanna's apartment and saw the filthy conditions in which she and her baby were living. He called the police, who contacted Child Protective Services to come and investigate. The social worker assigned to the case recognized that Connor was malnourished, and also saw that Deanna was psychologically disturbed because of her postpartum depression. The social worker made arrangements for Connor to be admitted to the hospital for medical help and for Deanna to see a psychiatrist. While he was in the hospital and being properly fed, Connor gained a pound a week until he was in the healthy weight range again. Deanna was prescribed antidepressants that helped bring her out of her depression, and she attended parenting classes provided by the county. Soon she was able to properly care for Connor while receiving welfare assistance to help her with her living expenses.

As can be seen in both of these examples, psychological maltreatment and neglect of children spans all regions of the socioeconomic spectrum. However, the underlying cause is the same–an inability to provide for the psychological or physical needs of the child. In the best case scenario, Trevor and Beth and their parents, through psychological counseling, would be able to form a more healthy and loving relationship that would be devoid of the insults, belittling, and ignoring of the children. As for our second example, with appropriate care and medical attention for both Connor and Deanna, as well as continued treatment of Deanna for postpartum depression and her moving on to a financially self-sufficient existence, Connor need never again experience the neglect and malnutrition that he experienced shortly after his birth.

Sexual Child Abuse

Alicia was eight years old when she began to avoid contact with all adults, especially men. She avoided her father, her friends' fathers, and even her schoolteacher Mr. Beckstrom—even though she really liked him. Being that Alicia was one of his favorite students, Mr. Beckstrom became concerned by the sudden change in Alicia's behavior, and asked that the school psychologist Dr. Thomas talk with Alicia in private. Alicia cried and cringed in the corner when she was alone with Dr. Thomas. After several meetings Alicia began to trust Dr. Thomas a little more and began to answer his questions, although she was still very nervous around him. He asked her "Has someone been hitting you?" and she replied "No." "Has someone been touching you somewhere they shouldn't?" asked Dr. Thomas. Alicia didn't reply, but Dr. Thomas noticed a look of fear in Alicia's face when he asked the question, and he immediately began to suspect sexual abuse. Dr. Thomas brought out a doll and asked Alicia to point to where she was touched. Alicia was hesitant at first, but eventually lifted the dress on the doll and pointed to where its private parts would be. In the next meeting with Alicia he asked her who had been touching her there, but Alicia refused to answer. "Was it your daddy?" Dr. Thomas asked, and Alicia froze in fear and began to cry, still refusing to answer. Given Alicia's response to the question about her father, and the fact that she particularly

Figure 7.1 President Clinton signs "Megan's Law" to establish a national database of sex offenders. © *AP Images*

avoided adult men, Dr. Thomas suspected that Alicia was being sexually abused by her father.

Most, if not all, societies in the world view child molestation and sexual abuse as heinous, deplorable, and cruel. Sexual child abuse leaves psychological scars on children that stay with them for the rest of their lives. Sexual abuse is enormously stressful to a child, both at the time it actually happens as well as for many years down the line. As such, victims of sexual abuse often end up with stress disorders such as PTSD.

HOW COMMON IS SEXUAL CHILD ABUSE?

The prevalence of sexual child abuse is extremely difficult to measure, mostly because it goes unreported almost 90 percent of the time.[10] In addition, abusive incidents often become repressed memories—the events are subconsciously "forgotten" for years—which also leads to a low rate of reporting. Other reasons for the low rate of reporting sexual child abuse include the fact that the abuse is difficult to prove (and easy to deny), the testimony of children is often considered less trustworthy than that of adults, and parents sometimes do not pursue the prosecution of abusers because of the stigma and negative attention they would attract, and the extreme hardships the child would have to face.

Regardless of the low report rates, a recent study by the World Health Organization (WHO) estimated that as many as 20 percent of adult women worldwide have been victims of sexual child abuse, and between 5 and 10 percent of adult men worldwide have been victims.[11] Sexual child abuse is generally less common than other forms of child abuse (including psychological maltreatment and neglect or physical child abuse). Only about 10 percent of maltreated children are victims of sexual abuse. Male children tend to be sexually abused at a much younger age (usually between the ages of 4 and 6 years) than female children (who are usually abused between the ages of 11 and 14),[12] perhaps because by the time male children become adolescents, they grow bigger and stronger than their potential abusers.

DEFINITION OF SEXUAL CHILD ABUSE

Sexual child abuse is defined broadly as sexual activity between an adult and a child that is initiated by the adult, and from which the adult receives some sort of sexual gratification. The sexual activity can include kissing (kissing on the lips for long periods of time or "tongue" kissing); touching or fondling the breasts, buttocks, or genitals; and sexual intercourse (vaginal, oral, or anal). When sexual intercourse is involved, it is usually coerced or forced, the latter of which is defined as rape. However, other behaviors that don't actually involve physical contact may be considered sexually abusive, such as exposing one's genitals to a child (flashing), photographing naked children for the purposes of pornography (exploitation), or graphic conversations with children about sex.

The sexual abuse of a child is not usually an isolated, one-time incident. It tends to progress gradually in several stages and often goes on for years. At first, the abuser gets to know the child (if he or she doesn't know the child already) and either tries to verbally convince the child to perform a sexual act (for example, by saying things like "all daddies do this with their children"). If the child does not cooperate, the abuser may force him or her into sexual activity by intimidation or physically overpowering the child. After the actual sexual activity, the abuser convinces the child to keep the events a secret through intimidation, blackmail, bribery, or other means. Often, this cycle of sexual abuse and secrecy goes on for years before it is disclosed—either by the child telling another adult about the abuse or the abuser being caught in the act. Because sexual child abuse carries an enormous psychological burden and social stigma, many times the parents of the child or the afflicted child does not report the abuse to the proper authorities.

SIGNS OF SEXUAL ABUSE

In small children who have limited communication skills, sexual abuse can lead the victim to have frightening dreams or even incorporate the sexual acts that have been done to them into play with dolls or other children. Some sexually abused children can direct their anger outward and become aggressive and show cruelty toward other kids. Others may direct their troubled feelings inward and become depressed or socially withdrawn. Some abused children even run away from home. In addition, sexually abused children may show seductive types of behavior (such as wearing makeup or revealing clothing) at an inappropriate age.

Childhood sexual abuse has tremendous effects on a child that last into adolescence and adulthood. Depression, anxiety, PTSD, emotional problems, poor self-esteem and body image distortions, and thoughts of suicide are common. Criminal behavior, self-destructive behavior (for example, intentionally cutting oneself with sharp objects), aggression, and drug and alcohol abuse are common. Abused children have difficulty trusting others (especially adults) and feel a tremendous amount of shame and guilt. In addition, adolescents or adults who were sexually abused as children often have trouble maintaining friendships and intimate relationships and may have anxieties or phobias associated with sex.

Not all children react to sexual abuse in the same way. The amount of trauma the child experiences depends on many variables. Factors that increase the degree of trauma include the abuser being a close family member, abuse that lasts for years, severe or physically damaging sexual abuse, the tendency of adults not to believe the child when he or she tells about the abuse, and the failure to report the abuse until later in adulthood. All of these factors tend to be seen in those people who are the most psychologically scarred by sexual abuse.

As with other forms of child abuse, factors that put a child at risk for sexual child abuse include isolation of the family from friends and social support networks, and the presence of domestic violence, divorce, or drug or alcohol abuse in the family.

CHARACTERISTICS OF PEOPLE WHO SEXUALLY ABUSE CHILDREN

About 60 percent of adults who commit sexual child abuse are nonrelatives who already know the child, such as a friend of the family, babysitter, or neighbor. Some 30 percent of sexual child abusers are family members of the child, such as parents, step-parents, older brothers or sisters, uncles, aunts, grandparents, or cousins. Only about 10 percent of child sexual abusers are complete strangers to the child.

The vast majority (an estimated 95 to 98 percent) of people who sexually abuse children are male, regardless of whether the abused child is male or female. Many sexual child abusers were victims of some sort of childhood abuse that may have been physical, psychological, or sexual in nature. As a result of their low self-esteem and their need for control in their lives that results from being abused, sexual child abusers satisfy their need for power by manipulating and controlling the children they abuse. Many sexual abusers of children also have strong interests in pornography and have a history of dysfunctional families and childhoods. However, none of these factors guarantees that a person will be a child molester. Some sexual abusers had normal childhoods.

People who are sexually interested in children are called **pedophiles**. Their sexual orientation is aimed exclusively at children. In many cases, a pedophile's sexual interest in children begins in adolescence and may be compulsive and uncontrollable. A **pederast** is an adult male who seeks out and engages in a consenting sexual relationship with an adolescent male despite the fact that minors are not legally able to give such consent. Because this practice is illegal in the United States, these individuals often pursue it through underground sex rings.

INCEST

Sexual activity between members of the same family, called **incest**, has been considered taboo for centuries. Even in biblical times, sexual activity between parents and their children was forbidden. Although raising a child often involves closeness and physical touching (such as hugs and kisses), some parents are not able to confine their physical intimacy with their children within appropriate limits.

The most common type of incest takes place between a father and his daughter. The incestuous father is most commonly described as someone who feels powerless and alienated from his wife and tries to overcome these feelings by establishing a rigid, dominating, and controlling sexual relationship with his daughter. The daughter is also plagued by low self-esteem and vulnerability. Sometimes, the mother may become aware of the relationship between her husband and

Megan's Law

A victory in the protection of children from sexual abuse occurred in 1996 when President Bill Clinton signed federal legislation (called "Megan's Law") to establish a national database of sex offenders. The bill was inspired by the mother of Megan Kanka, a New Jersey girl who was raped and murdered by a man who had previously been convicted of two cases of sexual assault. It turns out that Megan's killer was living with two other convicted sex offenders in the same apartment across the street from the Kanka family. Although convicted sex offenders have been required to register with local police departments for more than 50 years, information about their past was not available to the public until Megan's Law was passed. With the establishment of and public access to this national database on the criminal histories of convicted sex offenders and their current addresses, parents can now log onto daughter but withdraws from involvement and allows it to continue. Many daughters who have been victims of incest often feel as much resentment toward their mothers for not intervening as they do toward their fathers for sexually abusing them.

Aside from father-daughter incestuous relationships, there can also be father-son, mother-son, and mother-daughter sexual activity, and even incestuous relationships between siblings. These are, however, far less common than the father-daughter relationship. Uncles, aunts, cousins, and even grandparents can also commit acts of incest.

the Internet and learn whether any potential sex offenders are living in their neighborhood. In addition, in some states, police will alert local residents when a sex offender moves to their area.

Megan's Law is controversial. Some claim that while the law alerts people to previous sex offenders, it does nothing to protect children from someone who may be about to commit a first offense. Others believe it infringes on the sex offender's right to live in peace and continue his or her recovery. Sex offenders feel that they have to pay twice for their crime—once in jail and then again when they get out. However, sex offenders can be habitual offenders, and unless they seek treatment, they may continue their criminal behavior once released from prison. A recent study showed that sex offenders who do not undergo some sort of treatment are almost twice as likely to commit a repeat offense as those who do undergo treatment.[13]

Figure 7.2 A therapist uses toys as therapeutic tools with her child client. © *Blair Seitz/Photo Researchers, Inc.*

OTHER SEXUAL CHILD ABUSE SETTINGS

Recently, the media have given a lot of attention to cases of Catholic priests who have been accused of sexually molesting children in their church (such as altar boys). Despite this focus on the Catholic Church, sexual abuse can occur in any religious organization. It is believed that religious figures who engage in sexual child abuse do so out of their higher authority (not only within the organization's structure but also from his or her connection to God). On the other hand, some men who recognize their own misguided sexual desires for children seek out remediation by becoming celibate (sexually abstinent) and later give in to the temptation of engaging in sexual behavior with children.

Other stories in the media have highlighted cases of sexual abuse in day-care settings, such as the case of McMartin Preschool in California in the 1980s, where numerous children were sexually abused over a long period of time by day-care workers. Such instances have prompted tougher screening of workers and increased insurance rates at day care facilities.

The Internet has become one of the most widely used settings for child pornography and prostitution. Although some sexual child abusers use the Internet to view and post pornographic photographs of children (both male and female), others use online chat rooms to seek out and seduce children into sexual relationships. Because users of the Internet are largely anonymous and hard to track, arresting and prosecuting these individuals is extremely difficult.

INTERVENTION AND TREATMENT

As with other types of child abuse, the first step in intervention and treatment of sexual child abuse is stopping the abusive behavior. Since sexual behavior between adults and children in the United States is illegal, the abuser is usually arrested and prosecuted. If the abuse is not severe and the abuser is not jailed, the court may order that the abuser's family enter a treatment program, such as the Child Sexual Abuse Treatment Program located in California. Here, both the victim and the abuser can undergo counseling and psychotherapy. Younger children or children who do not feel comfortable talking about

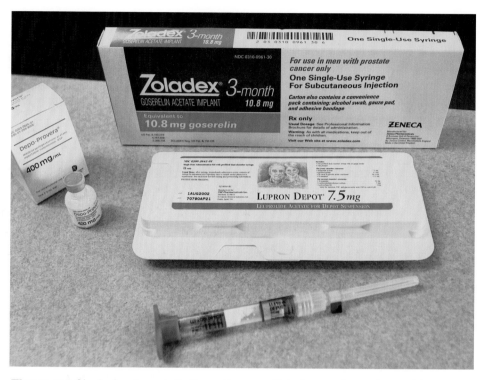

Figure 7.3 Clockwise from left, Depo Provera, Zoladex, and a syringe of Lupron, drugs used as part of the effort to control the deviant urges of sex offenders. © *AP Images*

their experiences may use art or play therapy to express their feelings.

During the first phases of treatment there may be a lot of denial, hostility, and anger between the victim and the abuser, and the victim may experience severe depression or suicidal thoughts. Once the victim accepts that abusive experiences are a part of history that cannot be changed, and the abuser accepts his or her responsibility for what happened, the therapist usually attempts to help the family focus on building a healthy future. The therapist may also assist in improving communication among family members and resetting generational boundaries (for example, emphasizing that sex should remain between a husband and his wife and not include other family members).

Intense psychotherapy is usually needed for the victim to help him or her overcome guilt, shame, poor self-esteem and self-image, difficulty with relationships, and lack of trust with others. Sometimes, if needed, medications such as antidepressants may be prescribed for the depression and anxiety that occur. The victim is taught to trust adults again and to manage his or her anger toward the abusive parent.

In treating the abusers, one of the first steps is to get them to accept responsibility for their actions and to stop the pattern of abuse. If the abuser is a pedophile and his or her sexual behavior toward children is compulsive, then extensive cognitive behavioral therapy is needed to redirect his or her sexual urges toward adults. Although the ultimate goal of any treatment is to reunite a happy and functional family, this is often not possible because the abuser is in prison, where therapy options are not as available. Many times, if the abuser cannot correct his or her sexual behavior, the courts will not allow him or her to return to the family. If the abuser becomes a repeat sex offender, biological deterrents such as **chemical castration** may be necessary (the man's testicles are inhibited or destroyed with hormones or other chemicals so they do not produce testosterone, the main hormone that regulates the male sex drive).

CASE STUDY

It wasn't until Marcus was in his early 30s that he discovered that he had been sexually abused as a child. He worked as an electrician and was married with two young children (both boys). His wife worked as a marketing director for a computer manufacturer. As his wife was promoted up through the ranks of her company, she began working longer hours, and the lack of attention he received from her made Marcus feel neglected and depressed.

To cope with his depression and need for attention, at night, after the rest of his family had gone to bed, Marcus would surf the Internet for pictures of preadolescent girls. Marcus found himself sexually aroused by the photographs that he found and, eventually, found his way to a chatroom where he could converse with children. One night, Marcus went out for a late-night drive to clear his mind and, while stopping at a convenience store, he saw the 13-year-old daughter of one of his regular customers, who had stopped in for some candy on her way home from a friend's house. He offered her a ride home, and since she knew Marcus from the work he had done at her parents' house, she accepted. As he drove he began to fantasize about having sex with the young girl. On a darkened road along the way, Marcus suddenly stopped the car and began to kiss the young girl and grab at her breasts. She eventually fought free and ran the rest of the way home, and told her parents about the incident. Marcus continued to drive around for a while, but by the time he returned home, the police were waiting for him.

Marcus was arrested and charged with sexual assault against a minor. When he was being interviewed by detectives, he confessed that he had done things like this before but had never gotten into trouble. Marcus stated that the relationships he initiated with young girls in person or over the Internet were more satisfying than his marriage was. Marcus also began to recall how his own father began sexually abusing him when he was in kindergarten. During that time, Marcus's father often came home from work drunk and, after everyone had gone to bed, would crawl into Marcus's bed with him and rub his genitals up against Marcus's buttocks.

After serving six months in jail for sexual assault, Marcus was released for good behavior and he returned home to his family. At his parole hearing, Marcus was ordered to undergo family therapy to improve his relationship with his wife and children and to help family communication. Marcus and his wife also saw a marriage counselor to work out Marcus's feelings of neglect due to his wife's success at work and her busy schedule. Finally, Marcus underwent intense psychotherapy to help deal with his sexual attraction to young girls and to redirect his sexual attraction toward adult women.

Like other forms of child abuse, sexual abuse has many causes and consequences. However, our society perceives sexual crimes, particularly those committed against children, to be particularly heinous and reprehensible. The psychological scars brought on by sexual child abuse are often permanent and cannot be undone with any amount of psychotherapy. However, with the proper help and resources, victims of childhood sexual abuse can lead normal, healthy, and productive lives.

8 Summary

Stress is a natural psychological and biological response to the demands that are placed on individuals by other people, events, diseases, or even themselves. Through stress people are able to focus on and react (either mentally or physically) to a certain situation. In times of stress, the body increases the production of stress hormones such as cortisol and adrenaline. In the short run, these molecules help the body react to stress by increasing attention levels and memory capabilities, diverting blood flow to vital organs and activating the immune system. However, when stress becomes chronic, the persistent increases in the levels of these molecules begin to become harmful to the body, putting it at risk for cardiovascular disease, susceptibility to infection, ulcers, depression, and even the loss of brain cells. Researchers who study stress are interested in determining not only the factors that put people at risk for developing stress-related health problems, but also ways of preventing or reversing these problems.

When people are faced with the severe stress of a traumatic event (such as a major earthquake, terrorist attack, being a victim of a violent crime, or loss of a loved one) the normal stress reaction can go awry and result in the development of stress disorders. Acute Stress Disorder and Post-Traumatic Stress Disorder are examples of disorders in which severe anxiety, flashbacks and avoidance of people or things related to the

traumatic event occur to such a degree that they are debilitating and interfere with daily functioning. Acute Stress Disorder
occurs within the first four weeks after the traumatic event,
and often evolves into Post-Traumatic Stress Disorder, when
the symptoms are present more than four weeks following the
event. Both disorders are most effectively treated with cognitive behavioral therapy, in which the patient is taught how to
reevaluate and reinterpret the traumatic event. This type of
therapy also provides a method of desensitizing a person to
the feelings of anxiety and avoidance of people, places, or
objects associated with the trauma. Cognitive behavioral therapy is sometimes combined with prescription medications
that help ease the anxiety, depression, and sleep disturbances
brought on by the trauma. Some researchers believe that
developing new ways of "learning to forget" traumatic events
would be greatly beneficial to the sufferers of stress disorders,
but others feel that through the appropriate type of therapy,
people can eventually gain strength and personal growth from
a traumatic event.

Children are especially vulnerable to the effects of trauma,
particularly when it comes in the form of physical, mental, or
sexual abuse from parents or other caregivers. Parents who
abuse or neglect their children can generally be described as
being self-absorbed and incapable of recognizing and provid-
ing for the emotional and physical needs of a child. Child
abuse often causes behavioral problems (aggression, defiance
of authority, drug and alcohol use, or even suicide) as well as
a host of emotional issues (depression, withdrawal, anger, and
distrust of others) that can last for years or even decades.
Many survivors of child abuse (particularly those who were
abused sexually or physically) have hyperactive stress responses and go on to develop Post-Traumatic Stress Disorder.
Prevention of child abuse is difficult since it usually happens

within the confines of a home. However, knowing the signs of child abuse can greatly improve the chances of reporting abuse, intervention, prosecution, and rehabilitation of abusers, and most importantly, the beginning of the healing process for the abused child.

1. Costello, E.J., S. N. Compton, G. Keeler, and A. Angold. "Relationships between poverty and psychopathology: a natural experiment." *Journal of the American Medical Association* 290 (2003): 2023–2029.
2. Wilson, S.H., and G.M. Walker. "Unemployment and health: a review." *Public Health* 107 (1997): 153–162.
3. Leor, J., W. K. Poole, and R. A. Kloner. "Sudden cardiac death triggered by an earthquake." *New England Journal of Medicine* 334 (1996): 413–419.
4. Glaser, R., J. Rice, J. Sheridan, R. Fertel, J. Stout, C. Speicher, D. Pinsky, M. Kotur, A. Post, M. Beck, et al. "Stress-related immune suppression: health implications." *Brain, Behavior and Immunity* 1 (1987): 7–20.
5. Spiegel, D., J. R. Bloom, H. C. Kraemer, and E. Gottheil. "Effect of psychosocial treatment on survival of patients with metastatic breast cancer." *The Lancet* 2, no. 8668 (1989): 888–891.
6. Posttraumatic Stress Disorder Alliance. "What is PTSD?" Available online. URL: http://www.ptsdalliance.org. Downloaded on June 5, 2006.
7. U.S. Department of Health and Human Services. *Child Maltreatment, 2004: Reports from the States to the National Child Abuse and Neglect Data System*, Washington, D.C.: U.S. Government Printing Office, 2006.
8. U.S. Department of Health and Human Services, Children's Bureau. *Child Maltreatment 1998.* Washington, D.C.: U.S. Government Printing Office, 2000.
9. van Cleve, T.C. *The Emperor Frederick II of Hohenstufen, Immutator Mundi.* Oxford: Oxford University Press, 1972.
10. Hanson, R. F., H. S. Resnick, B. E. Saunders, D. G. Kilpatrick, and C. Best. "Factors related to the reporting of childhood rape." *Child Abuse and Neglect* 23, no. 6 (1999): 559–569.
11. World Health Organization (WHO). *World Report on Violence and Health.* Geneva: WHO, 2002.
12. Whealin, J. "Child sexual abuse—a National Center for PTSD Fact Sheet." Available online. URL: http://www.ncptsd.va.gov/facts/specific/fs_child_sexual_abuse.html. Downloaded on April 19, 2006.
13. Hanson, R.K., A. Gordon, A. J. R. Harris, J. K. Marques, W. Murphy, V. L. Quinsey, and M. C. Seto. "First report of the Collaborative Outcome Data Project on the effectiveness of psychological treatment for sexual offenders." *Sexual Abuse: A Journal of Research and Treatment* 142 (2002): 169–194.

GLOSSARY

active coping—A strategy used in psychotherapy that encourages the patient to recognize and accept (rather than deny) the impact of a traumatic event, and teaches that the patient must take an active role in taking control over and improving his or her own life.

acute stress disorder—A mental disorder where symptoms such as flashbacks, severe anxiety, and depersonalization develop within 4 weeks after experiencing or witnessing a severely traumatic event. Often abbreviated ASD.

adrenaline—A hormone that is secreted by the adrenal glands and autonomic nervous system during stress that stimulates heart rate and breathing and increases blood pressure. Also called epinephrine.

adrenocorticotropin releasing hormone—During stress, this hormone is released from the pituitary gland into the bloodstream where it travels to the adrenal glands to stimulate the production of cortisol. Often abbreviated ACTH.

anxiety disorder—A mental disorder that includes excess or irrational fears of people, places, objects, or normal situations. ASD and PTSD are examples of anxiety disorders.

atherosclerosis—The process in which fats and other materials build up in the wall of blood vessels and cause them to thicken, clog, harden, and narrow, decreasing blood supply to specific organs or parts of the body.

attention deficit/hyperactivity disorder—A psychological disorder that primarily affects children. Children with ADHD are easily distracted from a task by sights and sounds, have difficulty concentrating for long periods of time, are restless and impulsive, are often slow to complete tasks, and have a tendency to daydream. Often abbreviated ADHD, and also known as attention deficit disorder (ADD).

autonomic nervous system—The part of the nervous system that controls involuntary actions, as of the cardiovascular and respiratory systems.

biofeedback—A technique used in the treatment of anxiety or other psychological disorders in which an individual learns to voluntarily control physiological measures which are normally under involuntary control, such heart rate, brain waves, and blood pressure. These measures are monitored electronically through sounds or graphs on a computer screen where they are displayed to the patient, and he or she learns to monitor and control his or her own physiological responses to anxiety-provoking ideas or situations. With enough training the individual can learn to control these physiological measures without the use of electronic equipment.

chemical castration—A method used by law enforcement agenices to reduce or eliminate sexual impulses in male sex offenders. Sex offenders are usually given a hormone pill that blocks the ability of the brain to send signals to the testicles to produce testosterone, the hormone that controls male sex drive. Unlike surgical castration, the reduced sexual impulses caused by chemical castration are not permanent.

cognitive behavioral therapy—A method of treating mental disorders based on identifying and correcting inaccurate thought processes associated with depressed or anxious feelings, encouraging people to engage more often in enjoyable activities, and increasing problem-solving skills. Abbreviated CBT.

cognitive style—A set of specific beliefs or way of thinking.

corticotrophin-releasing hormone—This hormone is released from the brain into the pituitary gland during stress. Also called corticotrophin-releasing factor, and abbreviated either CRH or CRF.

cortisol—A steroid molecule that is released by the adrenal glands into the bloodstream during stress.

depersonalization—The feeling that one's body or parts of one's body are not his or her own, or the feeling that one is looking at oneself from the outside. Also called an "out-of-body" experience.

depression—A mental disorder characterized by feelings of despair, guilt, loneliness, extreme sadness, and worthlessness. People who are depressed often experience disturbances in sleep patterns, fluctuations in weight, lethargy, difficulty concentrating, or decrease in libido. They may even have thoughts of death or suicide.

derealization—The feeling that one's surroundings are not real or are dream-like.

dissociative amnesia—An inability to recall certain events or occurrences after experiencing or witnessing a severely traumatic event.

dissociative symptoms—Symptoms of ASD or PTSD that make one feel dissociated from reality, such as feelings of numbness, detachment from everyday life, lack of emotional responses, amnesia, feeling as if one's body is not their own, or the perception that one's surroundings seem unreal or dreamlike.

fight-or-flight response—General term used for activation of the sympathetic division of the autonomic nervous system that readies the body to react to stress by increasing heart rate, blood pressure, blood flow to the brain and skeletal muscles, etc. Also called the alarm response.

flashback—A sudden but brief reexperience of a prior traumatic event.

gastrointestinal tract—Often called the GI tract, this system includes all parts of the digestive system, including the mouth, throat, esophagus, stomach, intestines, rectum and anus.

hippocampus—A region of the brain that is involved in the storage and retrieval of memories.

hypervigilance—The state of being overly watchful, cautious, jumpy, or on guard.

immune system—An organized network of specialized glands and cells in the body that help fight against infections and foreign organisms such as bacteria and viruses.

incest—Sexual relationships or activity between members of the same family.

interactional process—A process by which one factor interacts with another to produce an effect greater than either of the individual factors alone. For example, if a parent views his or her child as difficult and becomes stressed by the child's defiant behavior, the parent may lash out and strike the child. This, in turn, can make the child more resentful of the parent and subsequently more defiant.

irritable bowel syndrome—A disorder that is caused by overactivity of the nerves that control the muscles in the gastrointestinal tract, causing it to become overly sensitive to food, intestinal gas, and stress. The result is abdominal pain and cramping, "bloated" feelings, and frequent diarrhea or constipation. Often abbreviated IBS. Also called spastic colon or mucous colitis.

metabolism—The chemical and physical processes by which substances (such as food) are transformed into energy or other biological products for use by the body.

Munchausen syndrome—A psychological disorder in which an adult fakes an illness or harms his or herself intentionally in order to get attention from others, especially from medical or hospital staff. Also known as factitious disorder.

Munchausen syndrome by proxy—A psychological disorder in which a parent or caregiver intentionally harms his or her child in order to get attention from others, especially from medical or hospital staff.

negative feedback—The process by which the body senses increased levels of a substance (such as cortisol in the bloodstream) and reacts by decreasing the production of this substance.

neurotransmitter—Chemical messengers used by nerve cells in the brain and other parts of the nervous system. Neurotransmitters allow nerve cells to communicate with one another as well as with muscles and organs.

noradrenaline—A hormone secreted by the adrenal glands during stress that stimulates heart rate and breathing and increases blood pressure. Noradrenaline is also used as a chemical messenger by the nervous system. Also called norepinephrine.

nonorganic failure to thrive—A medical condition in infants characterized by slow growth and development and gastrointestinal problems, usually due to malnutrition. Often abbreviated NFTT.

parasympathetic division—The part of the autonomic nervous system that opposes the physiological effects of the sympathetic nervous system after a stress response by decreasing heart rate and blood pressure, contracting the pupils, etc.

pederast—An adult male who seeks out and engages in a consenting sexual relationship with an adolescent male.

pedophile—An adult who is sexually attracted to and oriented toward children.

pituitary gland—A gland that sits at the base of the brain that secretes numerous hormones of varying biological functions, including hormones associated with the stress response.

plaques—Deposits of fats and other materials that lodge in the walls of blood vessels that can narrow or even block off blood supply to an organ or part of the body.

platelets—Specialized cells in the blood that aid in clotting. Also called thrombocytes.

postpartum depression—A severe form of depression that affects women soon after childbirth. It is thought to be a result of significant hormonal changes that occur in the mother following the birth of an infant.

post-traumatic stress disorder—A mental disorder where symptoms such as flashbacks, severe anxiety, and depersonalization develop more than 4 weeks after experiencing or witnessing a severely traumatic event. Abbreviated PTSD.

progressive exposure therapy—A type of therapy for psychological problems or disorders, usually anxiety disorders, in which a person (under the supervision of a therapist) is introduced to people, places, or objects associated with a traumatic event in a gradual, progressive manner to confront, control, and desensitize anxious feelings. For example, a person traumatized by being attacked by a dog would first be shown pictures of a dog, then sounds of a dog barking, then be put in a room with a dog on a leash, then ultimately encouraged to pet the dog.

psychological maltreatment—A continuing pattern of parental behavior that is psychologically destructive to the child. Usually, it includes rejection, bullying/frightening, social isolation, or corruption of the child.

psychosocial dwarfism—A medical condition in children that results in slowed growth and development due to malnutrition that occurs after infancy. Sometimes abbreviated PSD.

psychosocial support—Psychological help or support given by means of group or family therapy or counseling.

relaxation therapy—A type of therapy used in the treatment of anxiety disorders in which a person is taught to recognize symptoms of anxiety as soon as they occur and how to counteract them by such techniques as taking deep breaths, mental focusing, meditation, or muscle relaxation techniques.

serotonin—A chemical messenger in the brain that controls mood, feelings of pleasure, and emotion.

shaken baby syndrome—General term for when infants are shaken violently in an attempt by the parent or caregiver to get them to behave properly or stop crying.

steroid—A class of molecules with a distinct chemical structure that allows them to pass easily in and out of the bloodstream as well as in and out of individual cells. Cortisol in an example of a steroid.

stress—The mental and physical response to demands (whether psychological or physiological) that are placed on an individual.

stressor—Any event, person, object, or force of nature that places a demand on an individual.

subdural hematoma—Bleeding that occurs on the surface of the brain just underneath the brain's protective lining. Usually a result of trauma to the head.

sudden infant death syndrome—An unexpected and unexplained death of an infant less that one year of age. Often abbreviated SIDS.

sympathetic division—The part of the autonomic nervous system that readies the body to react to stress by increasing heart rate and blood pressure, diverting blood flow toward the brain and skeletal muscles, dilating the pupils, etc.

type A personality—A collection of personality characteristics such as being intensely driven to succeed, always busy, impatient, irritable, and hostile toward others. May make one more prone to heart disease.

thymus gland—A gland that rests just above the heart that is responsible for producing immune cells.

ulcer—A lesion or opening in the skin or a mucous membrane, including the mouth, esophagus, stomach, and intestines. Ulcers are usually characterized by inflamed, irritated, tender, infected or dead tissue.

ventricular fibrillation—A condition in which the lower half of the heart (the ventricles) contract in a rapid, irregular, and chaotic manner which results in an inability of the heart to pump blood to the body.

virtual reality—A computer-based technology used in psychological therapy which allows the patient to interact with the projection of a three-dimensional environment through goggles, headphones and even a full bodysuit. In the context of PTSD, scenarios similar to a traumatic event that has been experienced can be viewed and interacted with so the patient learns to cope with the painful memories and feelings associated with the event.

General

Crosson-Tower, C. *Understanding Child Abuse and Neglect,* 6th Edition. Boston: Allyn and Bacon, 2005.

McEwen, B., and E. N. Lasley. *The End of Stress as We Know It.* Washington, D.C.: Joseph Henry Press, 2002.

Sapolsky, R.M. *Why Zebras Don't Get Ulcers—An Updated Guide to Stress, Stress-Related Disorders, and Coping.* New York: W.H. Freeman and Company, 1998.

Chapter 1

McEwen, B., ed. *Handbook of Physiology—Section 7: The Endocrine System. Volume IV—Coping with the Environment: Neural and Endocrine Mechanisms.* New York: Oxford University Press, 2001.

Chapter 2

Sapolsky, R.M. *Why Zebras Don't Get Ulcers—An Updated Guide to Stress, Stress-Related Disorders, and Coping.* New York: W.H. Freeman and Company, 1998.

Chapter 3

Bryant, R. A., and A. G. Harvey. "Acute stress disorder: a critical review of diagnostic issues." *Clinical Psychology Review* 17 (1997): 757-773.

Diagnostic and Statistical Manual of Mental Disorders, 4th Edition (DSM-IV). Washington, D.C.: American Psychiatric Association, 1994.

Harbert, K. "Acute Traumatic Stress." *Clinician Reviews* 12, no. 1 (2002): 50-57.

Marshall, R. D., R. Spitzer, and M. R. Liebowitz. "Review and critique of the new DSM-IV diagnosis of acute stress disorder." *American Journal of Psychiatry* 156, no. 11 (1999): 1677-1685.

Gibson, L.E. "Acute stress disorder." Available online. URL: http://www.ncptsd.va.gov/facts/specifics/fs_asd.html. Downloaded on April 19, 2006.

Chapter 4

Diagnostic and Statistical Manual of Mental Disorders, 4th Edition (DSM-IV). Washington, D.C.: American Psychiatric Association, 1994.

Williams, R. "The psychosocial consequences for children and young people who are exposed to terrorism, war, conflict and natural disasters." *Current Opinion in Psychiatry* 19, no. 4 (2006): 337-349.

Friedman, M.J. "Posttraumatic stress disorder—an overview." Available online. URL: http://www.ncptsd.va.gov/facts/general/fs_overview.htm. Downloaded on April 19, 2006.

Chapter 6

U.S. Department of Health and Human Services, Children's Bureau. *National Child Abuse and Neglect Data System*. Washington, D.C.: U.S. Government Printing Office, 2003.

Bolen, R. *Child Sexual Abuse.* New York: Plenum Press, 2001.

Crosson-Tower, C. *Understanding Child Abuse and Neglect,* 6th Edition. Boston: Allyn and Bacon, 2005.

McEwen, B., and E. N. Lasley. *The End of Stress as We Know It.* Washington D.C.: Joseph Henry Press, 2002.

Sapolsky, R.M. *Why Zebras Don't Get Ulcers—An Updated Guide to Stress, Stress-Related Disorders, and Coping.* New York: W.H. Freeman and Company, 1998.

Web Sites

National Clearinghouse on Child Abuse and Neglect

http://nccanch.acf.hhs.gov/index.cfm

Child Trauma Academy

http://www.childtrauma.org

National Center for PTSD

http://www.ncptsd.va.gov/

Trademarks

Ambien is a registered trademark of Sanofi-Synthelabo, Inc.; Klonopin is a registered trademark of Hoffman-La Roche Inc.; Lunesta is a registered trademark of Sepracor Inc.; Paxil is a registered trademark of GlaxoSmithKline; Prozac is a registered trademark of Eli Lilly and Company; Valium is a registered trademark of Roche Pharmaceuticals; Xanax is a registered trademark of Pfizer Inc.; Zoloft is a registered trademark of Pfizer Inc.

INDEX

acid production in stomach, 6
  and ulcer disease in chronic stress, 17–18
ACTH (adrenocorticotropin releasing hormone), 4, 5, 7, 94
active coping, 94
  in post-traumatic stress disorder, 48
acute stress disorder, 23–34, 90–91
  case study on, 28–30
  definition of, 23, 94
  diagnosis of, 26–28
  incidence and prevalence of, 25–26
  post-traumatic stress disorder after, 25–26, 28, 30, 37, 91
  post-traumatic stress disorder compared to, 25, 28, 36
  risk factors in, 26
  signs and symptoms of, 26–28, 36
  treatment of, 29–34, 91
Acute Stress Disorder Interview (ASDI), 26
Acute Stress Disorder Scale (ASDS), 26
ADD (attention deficit disorder), 55, 94
ADHD (attention deficit/hyperactivity disorder), 55, 94
adolescents
  physical abuse of, 58–59
  post-traumatic stress disorder in, 42–43
  sexual abuse of, 78, 81
adrenal glands in stress response, 4, 5
adrenaline, 6–10, 90, 94
adrenocorticotropin releasing hormone (ACTH), 4, 5, 7, 94
aggressive behavior
  of physically abused child, 57, 58, 59, 62
  of psychologically abused child, 69
  of sexually abused child, 79
alarm response, 6
American Psychiatric Association on post-traumatic stress disorder, 37, 39
amnesia, dissociative, 27, 28, 95
anger
  of abusive parent or caregiver, 59, 60, 61
  of physically abused child, 57, 58, 63, 64

  in post-traumatic stress disorder, 49
  of sexually abused child, 79
anxiety disorder, 94
  acute stress disorder as, 28
Anxiety Disorders Interview Schedule (ADIS), 40
ASD. See acute stress disorder
Asian tsunami (December 2004), 2, 35, 36
atherosclerosis, 14, 94
attention deficit disorder, 55, 94
attention deficit/hyperactivity disorder, 94
  physical abuse of child with, 55
autonomic nervous system, 94
  parasympathetic division, 9, 97
  sympathetic division, 6, 20, 99

battle fatigue, 37
biofeedback, 33
  in acute stress disorder, 31–33
  definition of, 94–95
  in post-traumatic stress disorder, 47, 48
biology of stress response, 3–10, 90
  adrenaline in, 6–10, 90, 94
  cortisol in, 4–6, 90. See also cortisol
blood pressure
  biofeedback on, 32
  in initial stress response, 6, 9, 14
  in post-traumatic stress disorder, 41, 48
breast cancer, 16
bruises in abused child, 55

cancer, 16–17
Cannon, Walter, 2
caregivers. See parents and caregivers
case studies
  on acute stress disorder, 28–30
  on mental child abuse and neglect, 72–75
  on physical child abuse, 62–63
  on post-traumatic stress disorder, 44–46
  on sexual child abuse, 87–89
chemical castration, 87, 95

acute stress disorder compared to, 25, 28, 36

acute stress disorder prior to, 25–26, 28, 30, 37, 91

case study on, 44–46

in children and adolescents, 42–43

chronic, 40

definition of, 35, 98

delayed onset, 40

diagnosis of, 28, 39–41

historical descriptions of, 36–37

incidence and prevalence of, 37, 47

in children and adolescents, 43

myths on, 49–50

in physical abuse, 91

risk factors for, 38

in children and adolescents, 43

in sexual abuse, 77, 80, 91

symptoms of, 25, 28, 36, 39–41

in children and adolescents, 43

treatment of, 46–49, 91

in case study, 45–46

in children and adolescents, 43

ineffective approaches, 48–49

poverty, 13–14

mental child abuse and neglect in, 68

physical child abuse in, 54

progressive exposure therapy, 98

in acute stress disorder, 30, 31

in post-traumatic stress disorder, 45, 46–47

psychological debriefing in post-traumatic stress disorder, 46

psychological maltreatment, 65–75, 98. *See also* mental child abuse and neglect

psychosocial dwarfism, 69, 98

psychosocial support, 98

PTSD. *See* post-traumatic stress disorder

PTSD Checklist (PCL), 40

PTSD Symptom Scale Interview (PSS-I), 40

punishment of children, physical, 53

rape, 79

rejection feelings in mental abuse and neglect, 67

relaxation techniques, 98–99

in acute stress disorder, 31, 32

biofeedback in, 32, 33

in post-traumatic stress disorder, 47

religious settings, sexual abuse in, 84–85

self-esteem

of physically abused child, 57, 59, 62, 63

of physically abusive parent or caregiver, 60

of psychologically abused child, 69, 73

of sexual child abuser, 81

of sexually abused child, 80, 82, 87

Selye, Hans, 6, 7, 15, 17

serotonin, 21, 99

sexual child abuse, 76–89, 91

case study on, 87–89

characteristics of abuser in, 80–81

in day-care settings, 85

definition of, 78–79

incidence and prevalence of, 52, 77–78

Internet in, 85, 88

intervention and treatment in, 85–87

Megan's law on, 77, 82–83

national database on, 82–83

in religious settings, 84–85

reporting of, 77–78, 79, 85

risk factors for, 80

signs and symptoms of, 79–80

shaken baby syndrome, 57, 99

shell shock, 28, 37, 42

siblings

physical abuse of, 60

sexual abuse of, 81, 83

sleeping difficulties in acute stress disorder, 34

socioeconomic factors in stress, 12–14

and mental child abuse and neglect, 65, 68

and physical child abuse, 54
spastic colon (irritable bowel syndrome), 18, 96
Spiegel, David, 16
spousal abuse, 55, 60
steroids, 4–6, 99
    cortisol. *See* cortisol
stress
    acute disorder, 23–34. *See also* acute stress disorder
    adrenaline in, 6–10, 90, 94
    causes of, 11–14
    chronic, 11–22. *See also* chronic stress
    cortisol in, 4–6. *See also* cortisol
    definitions of, 1–3, 99
    health effects of, 11–22. *See also* health effects of stress
    mental child abuse and neglect in, 65, 68
    physical child abuse in, 54–55, 59–60, 61
    physiological changes in, 3–10
    positive effects of, 11
    post-traumatic disorder, 35–50. *See also* post-traumatic stress disorder
    socioeconomic factors in, 12–14, 54, 65, 68
stressors, 3, 11–14
    in acute stress disorder, 25
    categories of, 9
    definition of, 99
    socioeconomic, 12–14, 54, 65, 68
Structured Interview for PTSD (SI-PTSD), 40
subdural hematoma, 57, 99
substance abuse
    of parents or caregivers, 60, 68, 69
    of physically abused child, 64
    in post-traumatic stress disorder, 48
    of psychologically abused child, 69, 73
sudden infant death syndrome, 59, 99
suicidal behavior of sexually abused child, 80, 86
sympathetic nervous system, 6, 20, 99

terrorist attacks of September 11, 2001, 2, 19, 24
    and acute stress disorders, 23
    and post-traumatic stress disorder, 41
terrorization in mental abuse and neglect, 67
thymus gland, 99
    and immune function in chronic stress, 15–16
toilet training
    physical abuse affecting, 57, 58, 61, 62
    post-traumatic stress disorder affecting, 43
toys as therapeutic tools for sexually abused child, 84
tsunami in Asia (December 2004), 2, 35, 36
type A personality, 12, 99

ulcers, gastrointestinal
    in chronic stress, 17–18
    definition of, 99
    in post-traumatic stress disorder, 41

ventricular fibrillation, 14–15, 99
verbal child abuse. *See* mental child abuse and neglect
Vietnam veterans, post-traumatic stress disorder in, 37
virtual reality, 100
    in post-traumatic stress disorder therapy, 47–48, 100

Warren, Robin, 18
war veterans, post-traumatic stress disorder in, 37, 46
    case study on, 44–46
    incidence of, 47
    virtual reality combat simulators in, 47–48, 100
World Health Organization on prevalence of sexual child abuse, 78

M. Foster Olive received his bachelor's degree in psychology from the University of California at San Diego, and went on to receive his Ph.D. in neuroscience from UCLA. He is currently an assistant professor at the Center for Drug and Alcohol Programs and Department of Psychiatry and Behavioral Sciences at the Medical University of South Carolina. His research focuses on the neurobiology of addiction, and his work has been published in numerous academic journals, including *Psychopharmacology* and *The Journal of Neuroscience.*